The Middle Ages

Roy Burrell

Oxford University Press by arrangement with the British Broadcasting Corporation

© Roy Burrell 1980

First published 1980
Reprinted 1981 (twice), 1982, 1983, 1984, 1985

ISBN 0 19 918120 9

Oxford University Press, Walton Street, Oxford OX2 6DP

Oxford New York Toronto
Delhi Bombay Calcutta Madras Karachi
Petaling Jaya Singapore Hong Kong Tokyo
Nairobi Dar es Salaam Cape Town
Melbourne Auckland

and associated companies in
Beirut Berlin Ibadan Nicosia

Oxford is a trade mark of Oxford University Press

Typesetting by Tradespools Ltd., Frome, Somerset
Printed in Hong Kong

Contents

Chapter One   Norman England

1 William's Children

William   Robert   William Rufus   Henry   Adela

William the Conqueror's family was not a happy one. Richard, the first born, was killed in a hunting accident. William did not think too highly of Robert, the next oldest. He made Robert Duke of Normandy. He told his third son, also called William, that he was to be England's next king. He had one more son, Henry, and several daughters, one of whom was named Adela.

Robert rebelled against his father and had to be put in his place. It nearly went the other way. Robert and King William met in single combat in Normandy. William rode at his son but was knocked out of the saddle. Robert stood over him with drawn sword. William had to be rescued by one of his knights. When tempers had cooled, the two men made up their quarrel – but only for a time.

King William went back to Normandy again in 1087 to punish a French attack on his lands. He was nearly sixty. He captured the town of Mantes and had it burnt to the ground. As he rode through the ruins, his horse trod on a hot cinder and stumbled. William was thrown hard against the pommel of his saddle. He died of his injuries.

Robert had to be content with Normandy, while his younger brother William became King of England. William II had a nickname. People called him 'Rufus', which means 'red'. The name may have been given to him because he had a red face. He also had a hot temper. When something annoyed him, his face went scarlet. He was cruel and greedy too.

He even made money out of the Church. The Church had a great deal of land but when there was no bishop to receive the rent money, it went to the king. When a bishop or an abbot died, it was up to the king to pick a new man to take his place.

Rufus often pretended he couldn't make up his mind. The longer he delayed, the more rent money he could keep. After Archbishop Lanfranc died, the king would not name a new Archbishop of Canterbury for nearly five years. Then he only chose Anselm because he thought he was dying. He wasn't.

Rufus was always breaking his promises. He told the people of England he would make things easier for them. He swore to make punishments less cruel, but he made them even harsher. William the Conqueror had done away with hanging for some offences. Rufus brought it back. William the Conqueror had fenced off huge areas of forest for his favourite pastime of hunting. Some peasants had been hanged for daring to trap small animals there. Others had been turned off their land. Rufus gave his word that these peasants could have their lands back again. He broke his word.

In 1100 he was killed in the New Forest by an arrow. The king's body was found by a charcoal-burner. His death was said to be an accident but no one tried very hard to find out what had really happened.

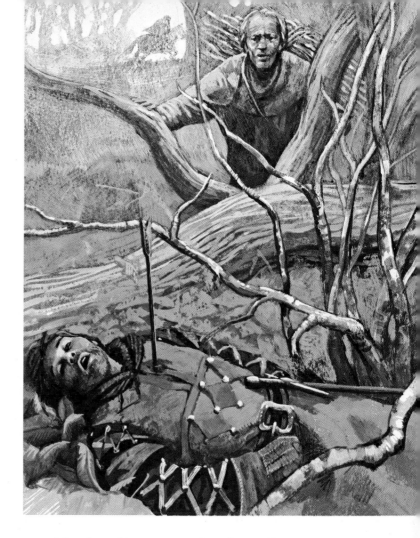

The Rufus Stone

The king's younger brother, Henry, was hunting in another part of the same forest. Henry didn't stop to find out the facts either. He galloped off to Winchester, took charge of the royal treasure and had himself proclaimed king.

Robert, Duke of Normandy, was very angry. He thought his younger brother Henry had cheated him of the crown. He stirred up trouble in both France and England. Henry crossed to Normandy, fought against his elder brother and captured him. Robert was held prisoner for the rest of his life, a period of 28 years. He was 80 when he died.

2 A Village Year

Spring

Winter

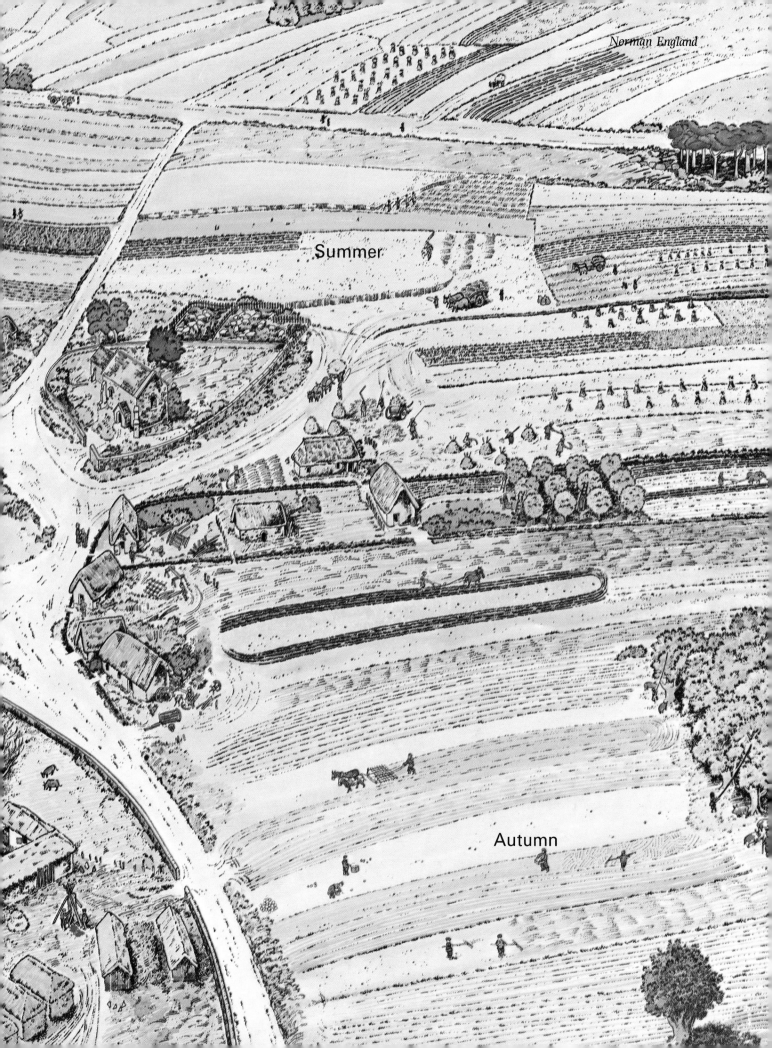

Summer

Autumn

3 A Town

St. George's Tower today

The castle mound today

The Northgate Tower today

4 The New Church

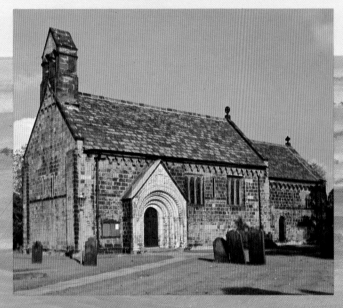

This is the church at Adel, near Leeds, in Yorkshire. Most of what you can see now was built in Norman times. Norman building methods were different from those of the Saxons. You can compare the picture of Adel Church with that of the Saxon church below. The large picture shows what Adel church must have looked like as it neared completion.

DAN ESCOTT

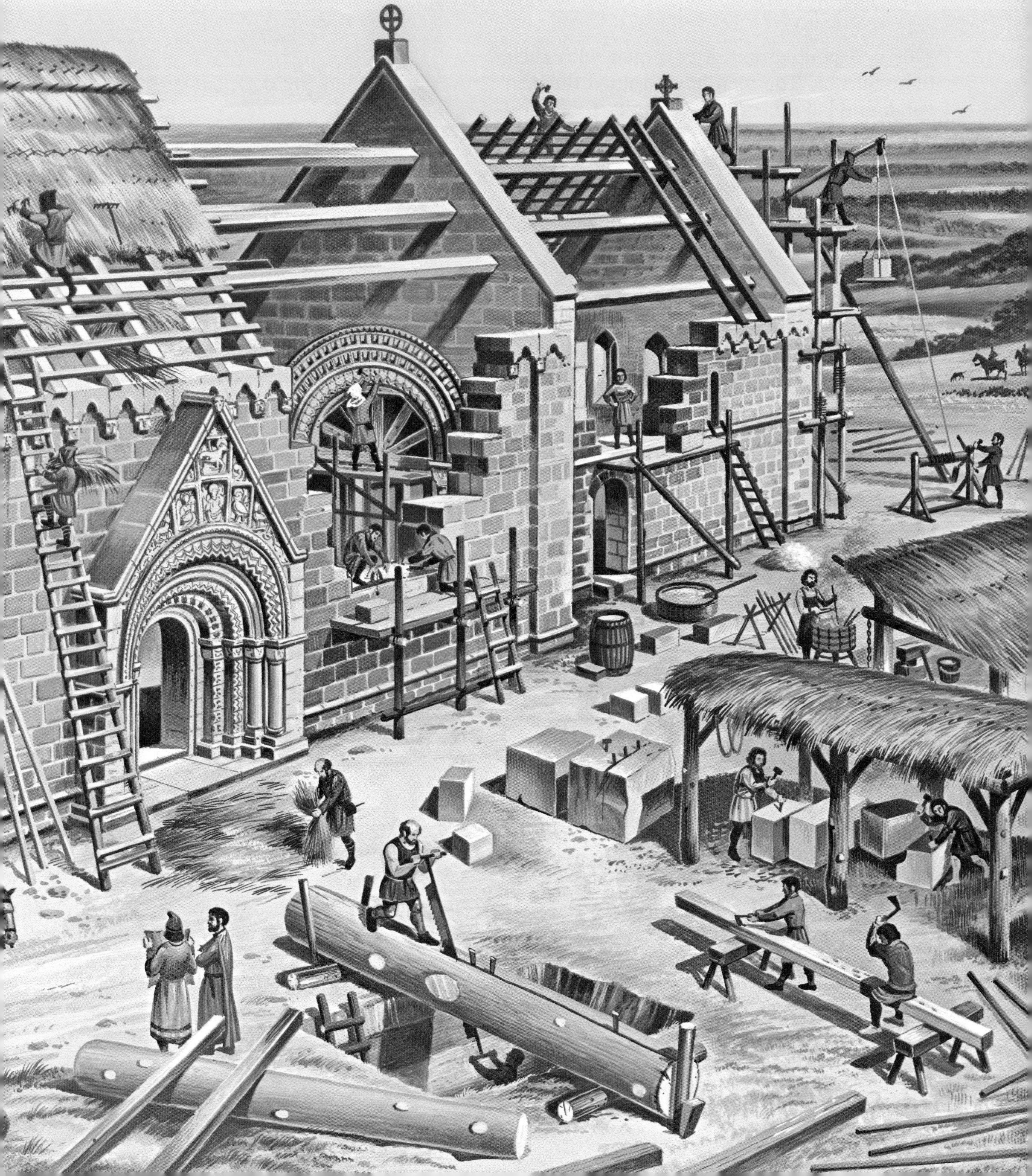

5 Hunting and Hawking

This is a photograph of two men with their tame falcons. The men have trained them to catch and kill other birds. Seagulls, rooks and sparrows flock around rubbish tips, looking for things to eat. If there is an airfield nearby they are often a danger to planes. There are cases of planes crashing after colliding with birds in mid air.

It's strange to think of something which began as a way for Man to get more food ending up as a scheme to cut down air crashes. In Norman times, falconry had already become a sport. Hunting of all kinds kept the Normans fit for fighting.

In the England of nine hundred years ago there was plenty of woodland in which to hunt. Much of the country was covered with forest. There were many wild animals. From the reign of William the Conqueror onward, large parts of England were fenced off as royal forests. Hardly a region was free of them. The most famous was the New Forest. Almost all of Essex was a game preserve and there were well over a dozen others. The king's keepers patrolled the areas looking for poachers. Poachers were punished by hanging.

The creatures hunted for food included wild boars, hares, rabbits and several kinds of deer. They were hunted with dogs specially bred for the chase. There were mastiffs, greyhounds, spaniels and terriers. The larger animals were followed on horseback and the smaller ones on foot.

For stag hunting, the party moved out into the country early in the morning. They took food and wine with them and had a picnic while men cast about with the dogs for the scent.

A hooded falcon   Falconer's gear

Horns were blown as soon as the dogs picked up the traces of a stag. The hunting party mounted their horses and galloped off. The servants used the dogs to drive the animal into a clearing where the hunters fired arrows at it or finished it off with spears.

Hares were usually driven into traps or nets by greyhounds. If they were hiding in a cornfield, the dogs flushed them out and the hunters shot at them with crossbows.

As we have seen, a favourite sport was hawking or falconry. In the wild, hawks catch small mammals or other birds. They hover until they see their prey. Then they swoop down on it and kill it with their claws.

From the earliest times, Man had learned to tame hawks. He trained them to kill and then return to his wrist with the prey. The falconer wore a leather glove because his bird's claws were both strong and sharp. The falcon tended to get excited if it saw anything worth chasing, so the falconer put a little leather hood over its head until the right prey appeared. Favourite targets were ducks, pigeons, partridges or geese.

Women went hunting with their menfolk sometimes. Anything that could be caught would be welcome, especially in winter, when fresh food was scarce.

13

6 Stephen and Matilda

Adela

Stephen and his seal

Matilda and her seal

Henry I

Before he died, King Henry I had to decide who was to be the next ruler. In those days, a leader was expected to fight battles, so a man was almost always chosen. The death of his son had left Henry with only one child, a daughter named Matilda. He made everyone promise to accept her as queen after his death.

Poor Matilda! When her cousin Stephen claimed the throne, all the promises were forgotten. The churchmen and most of the barons said that they would have him as their next king.

A civil war broke out which was to last for years. The barons tried hard to make sure that their own lands, titles and castles were safe. When it looked as if Matilda's followers were winning, some of Stephen's men changed sides. The opposite also happened. One or two of the barons changed sides several times.

At one stage, Stephen ruled his half of the country from London, while Matilda made

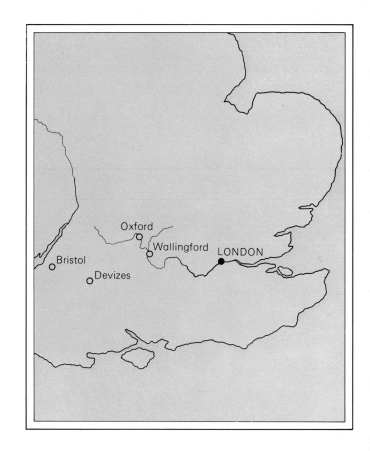

Bristol
Oxford
Wallingford LONDON
Devizes

Devizes in Wiltshire her capital. In 1141, the queen's army fought a battle and Stephen was taken prisoner. He was thrown into the dungeons of Bristol Castle.

Matilda thought she had won the war but it wasn't as easy as that. She entered London but the Londoners drove her out again. It seemed that quite a lot of people didn't care much for either Stephen or Matilda, and the war went on.

7 Nineteen Long Winters

Not every part of England suffered. In some areas the peasants hardly noticed that there was a war on at all. In other places the peasants knew only too well. Their lands became battlefields. Their animals and crops were destroyed. When that happened, they faced starvation.

A monk from Peterborough wrote an account of what life was like in the Fenlands near his monastery. If we could ask him about it, he might say something like this.

'Even if there is no battle, ordinary people can still be ruined. It happens when the local lord takes advantage of the breakdown in law and order and behaves like a robber baron.

'He recruits farm-hands into his private army and even brings soldiers over from Normandy or France. His officers lead them on raids against the lands of other barons. To pay

their wages, he makes his own tenants give him more and more in taxes.

'He arrests all the men who can't or won't pay and tortures them. His soldiers drive the animals off the farms and take the corn without payment or permission. If the robber baron suspects that someone has money hidden, the victim might be thrown into a dungeon until he tells where it is. The dungeon is sometimes known as an oubliette.

'Not only do the robber barons strike terror into the hearts of all the common people nearby, they are a menace to everyone from the ruler downwards. No one knows how he stands, for a once friendly baron can change sides overnight.

'Almost all the powerful barons have built new castles and filled them with evil men and devils. Thousands have been starved and tortured for their savings.

An oubliette

Peasants are taxed until they have nothing left. When they can pay no more, soldiers burn their villages as an example to others.

'You can go a whole day's journey and not see a village with a person alive nor any field being tilled. Food is so scarce and dear, that men who were once rich are now begging.

'Even when a few peasants do return to their homes, they can't make a living because the soil has been ruined. It seems as though it is winter all the time.'

The monk ended his chronicle with the following words: 'And so it lasted for nineteen years while Stephen was king, 'til the land was all undone and darkened with such deeds, and men said openly that Christ and his angels slept.'

Part of the monk's chronicle

8 Escape from Oxford

A surviving tower of Oxford Castle

After she was driven from London, Matilda decided to move to the west of England where she had more supporters. Unluckily for her, Robert, her half-brother, was captured by the other side. To ransom him, she had to let Stephen go. Many barons who had come over to Matilda when Stephen was first taken prisoner, now went back to him.

At one point, Matilda found herself in Oxford Castle surrounded by an enemy army. The besiegers tried to break in but the castle was too strong. They put up their tents, lit their fires and got ready for a lengthy siege. The well in the bailey of the castle would go on supplying water but food stores, however large, would not last for ever.

The siege went on through the autumn and into the winter. The weather turned cold and snow began to fall. At last the defenders could hold out no longer. Matilda decided that she must try to get away.

She held a meeting with her officers to discuss how she could escape. The constable of the castle had an idea. 'You can't go out through the main gate,' he said. 'Your only chance is to climb down one of the towers at the back of the castle where they won't be expecting anything to happen.'

Matilda didn't think she could climb down the wall so it was decided to lower her on a rope. Three of her knights were to go with her. One of her ladies came up with an idea as well. 'Your Majesty,' she said, 'if you try to cross the fields in those bright clothes you will be seen at once. May I suggest that long, white cloaks are made to cover you and your men completely? Then you won't stand out against the snow.'

The arrangements were made and at about midnight, a sentry signalled that all was clear. The three knights swarmed down the rope and waited at the bottom for the queen to be lowered. Silently, the four picked their way carefully across the frozen moat. The rope was drawn up and they were on their own.

Dodging and hiding, they made their way to the bank of the River Thames. Crossing the moat had been easy but would the ice of the river bear their weight? They thought it would be better to cross one at a time, first making as sure as they could that there was no one about.

The ice crackled warningly under their feet but it held. After what seemed like hours, they reached the far bank and began to feel a little safer.

They had some miles to go before they could get horses. They daren't try to get them while they were still so near Oxford. It started to snow again. This was lucky in one way because their tracks would be covered. But the queen was already exhausted and half-frozen. Finally, they found a lonely barn in which to spend the rest of the night.

The next morning, the men hired horses for themselves and a litter for Matilda. She was so ill she had to be lifted off it when they came at last to Wallingford Castle. Matilda recovered from her ordeal but her cause was getting nowhere until she let her son Henry take over the fight.

The war went on for several years but the end came suddenly and rather strangely. In 1153, Stephen was forced to sign an agreement which said that he should be king for the rest of his life but that Matilda's son should take the throne after him. Stephen had wanted his own son, Eustace, to succeed him, so it was with a heavy heart that he put his seal on the treaty. It didn't really matter. The next year Eustace died and Stephen followed him a few weeks later.

Matilda's son was crowned as Henry II.

Work Section

Understand your Work

1 William's Children
1 What is another way of saying 'first-born'?
2 Why didn't Robert become king when William the Conqueror died?
3 How many children did William have?
4 What is the 'pommel' of a saddle?
5 Why didn't William Rufus appoint a new archbishop straight away?
6 What does 'offences' mean?
7 Where was the royal treasure kept?
8 Why was Robert angry with Henry?
9 Who, do you think, are the three figures in the picture at the top of page 5?
10 Look at the photograph of the tomb on page 5. How did this Duke of Normandy come to be buried in Gloucester Cathedral?

5 Hunting and Hawking
1 What kinds of birds flock around rubbish tips?
2 Why are birds a danger to aeroplanes?
3 What is a poacher?
4 How were poachers punished in medieval times?
5 Which animals were hunted for food?
6 Which people looked for the tracks of the animals to be hunted?
7 What do wild hawks eat?
8 Which birds did the hawks kill?
9 Do modern falconers wear or use any items that would have been used in the Middle Ages?
10 Describe the scene in the picture at the top of page 13.

6 Stephen and Matilda
1 Why was the monarch usually a man?
2 Why didn't King Henry's son become king?
3 Who claimed the throne from Matilda?
4 What is a 'civil war'?
5 Which town did Matilda make her capital?
6 What happened in the year 1141?
7 Who did the people of London support in 1141?
8 Did the war end after the battle in 1141?
9 Look at the four people on page 14. Are they related to one another? Who was the grandfather of the two children?
10 Describe what is happening in the picture on page 15.

7 Nineteen Long Winters
1 Was everybody in England involved in the civil war?
2 In what ways did some farmers suffer?
3 Where are the fenlands?
4 What is a 'breakdown in law and order'?
5 What is an oubliette?
6 What happened to the peasants when they could no longer pay taxes?
7 What does 'tilled' mean?
8 Why were many rich people ruined?
9 Look at the manuscript on page 17. In which language is it written?
10 Look at the picture on page 17. These houses could be burned down much more easily than our own. Why was this?

8 Escape from Oxford
1 Which of Matilda's relations was captured?
2 Is there still a castle at Oxford?
3 What is a half-brother?
4 Why couldn't Matilda's enemies get into the castle?
5 Why was Matilda advised to wear a white cloak?
6 Why was it more difficult to cross the River Thames than the castle moat?
7 Who took over the command of Matilda's army?
8 Why didn't Stephen's son ever become king?
9 Look at the picture on page 19. What is the next obstacle the four characters will face? Can you see any signs of the enemy in the picture?

Use your Imagination

1 Imagine you are the charcoal-burner who found King William II's body. Describe what happened to a friend.
2 Imagine you are Robert, Duke of Normandy. Explain why you feel you have a better right to the English throne than your brother, Henry.
3 Imagine you live in the village shown on pages 6 and 7. Give a friend a guided tour of your village and describe the things you see.
4 The picture shows village life in spring, summer, autumn and winter. Describe the jobs the villagers do in each of the seasons.
5 What are the main differences between the town shown on pages 8 and 9 and the village shown on pages 6 and 7?
6 Try to imagine what your own town looked like in medieval times and describe it.
7 Look at the picture of the church on pages 10 and 11. Imagine you are the master mason who has to build Adel church. Describe to a visitor how a church is built.
8 What animals are hunted and sold for food today?
9 Imagine you are a medieval poacher. Why do you do it? What are the dangers and rewards? Do you consider that this form of stealing is wrong?
10 Do you think there are still poachers today?
11 In a civil war, what are the dangers of changing sides many times?
12 You are either Stephen or Matilda. What arguments can you use to persuade people to fight for you?
13 Imagine you have been thrown into an oubliette. Describe how you feel. What do you think will happen to you?
14 Explain what the Monk of Peterborough meant when he wrote, 'Men said openly that Christ and his angels slept.'
15 There have been many stories about 'great escapes'. Can you think of any? Why do you think escape stories are so popular?
16 Matilda and her companions wore white cloaks so they would not be seen against the snow. What sort of camouflages might be used in other surroundings such as deserts, forests and mountains?
17 Can you work out which town is shown on pages 8 and 9?

Further Work

1 Make a copy of William's family tree. Make one for your own family. Who in your group or class can go back the furthest?
2 If you live near enough, visit Duke Robert's tomb at Gloucester Cathedral, or the place in the New Forest where William II was shot.
3 Find your nearest Norman building. Describe it and, if possible, sketch it.
4 Find out what a charcoal-burner did. Why was his trade important? Why are there no charcoal-burners today?
5 Try to discover what sort of names the inhabitants on pages 6 and 7 may have had. Which of the names in your own class could they not have had?
6 Do people still have to hunt animals for food? Why do people still go hunting and what do they hunt?
7 Make a list of the mammals which still live wild in Britain.
8 Find out how and why rabbits were brought to Britain. What was the medieval name for a rabbit? What did the word rabbit mean in medieval times?
9 Find out all you can about the armour and weapons used during the reign of Stephen and Matilda. It's best to visit your local museum. Make sketches of what you find.
10 Collect pictures and make sketches of the sort of clothes worn in the days of Stephen and Matilda.
11 The barons did not want a woman as ruler of England. Why do you think this was? How many other women rulers of this country have there been? Were their reigns a success?
12 Find out how Henry I's son died. Retell the story of his death.

Chapter Two   Monastic Life

1 Monasteries

Eustace, the son of King Stephen, died in a monastery at Bury St. Edmunds. A monastery was the only place for sick people in those days. There were no state hospitals then.

Care of the sick was not the only task monasteries had. They looked after the poor by giving them bread when times were hard. They ran schools for the brighter children. They repaired roads and bridges. They provided beds and food for travellers. They kept learning and order alive in an age of ignorance and lawlessness.

Monasteries and nunneries were not founded just to do these things, though. They were places where people could devote

The main monasteries of England and Wales

Eustace on his death-bed

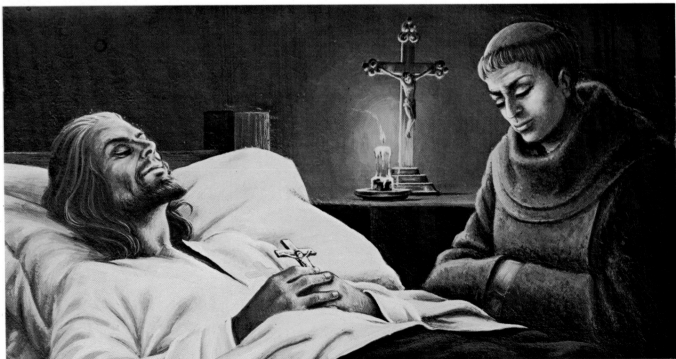

The fish that the monks caught was an important source of food for the monastery.

A monastic school

their whole lives to the worship of God. Nor were they new in Henry II's reign. They have a very long history.

The three main rules the monks followed were the vows of poverty, chastity and obedience. What did these things mean? Monks and nuns had to get rid of all their worldly possessions and promise not to own anything again. They vowed never to marry and always to do what they were told by those set over them.

Very often abbeys and convents had been founded by kings or members of their families. They had allowed the monks to build a chapel and somewhere to live. Lands had been given to them. The monks were expected to do a good deal of the work themselves but they still needed money. The rents from the lands were to help with the expenses.

As the years went by, a lot of abbeys found themselves getting richer as wealthy men and women left them lands and estates in their wills. St. Edmund's Abbey was already more than two and a half centuries old by the time a man called Jocelyn of Brakelonde became a monk. It covered a large area, even at that date.

23

2 Jocelyn of Brakelonde

In the British Museum there is a copy of a book written by Jocelyn. He was a monk at Bury St. Edmunds in the reign of Henry II. His book was a kind of diary. Have you ever kept a diary? Did you make up your mind that you would write in it every day? Jocelyn kept his diary going for nearly thirty years.

He probably made short notes which he then turned into a book. We don't know for certain he did this. We don't even have the book, let alone the notes. The copy we have was made by another monk about a hundred years after Jocelyn's death.

It is a history of his abbey, or monastery, from 1173 until the first year or two of the next century. It was mostly about the abbot, whose name was Samson. Jocelyn disagreed with the way Samson ran the abbey. Jocelyn was at great pains to let the monks know what property the abbey owned and what rights they were supposed to have. Because of his vow of obedience, he felt he could not openly defy Abbot Samson. He hoped that if he wrote down everything that had happened, those who came after him would not let their rights be taken away.

It may seem strange to us that Jocelyn was so concerned about property, that is to say buildings, farms, land, villages and so on. Surely this is not what is meant by poverty? Of course, Jocelyn did not have any possessions himself; it was the abbey which owned everything. Here is a picture of Jocelyn's abbey.

3 People of the Abbey

4 A Day in the Abbey

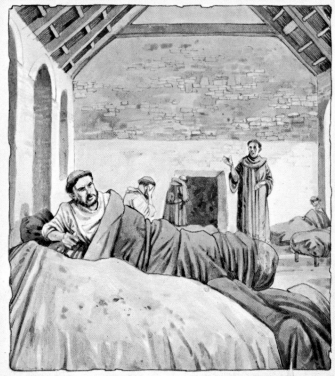

Time	Service or Activity	Place
Midnight	Matins	Church
1.00 a.m.	Lauds	Church
5.45 a.m.		
6.00 a.m.	Prime	Church
6.30 a.m.	Mass	Church
	Breakfast	Refectory
7.00 a.m.	Reading	Cloister
8.00 a.m.	Terce	Church
9.00 a.m.	Meeting	Chapterhouse
9.30 a.m.	Conversation	Cloister
10.00 a.m.	High Mass	Church
10.50 a.m.	Hand washing	Lavatory
11.00 a.m.	Dinner	Refectory
11.30 a.m.	Rest period	
12.30 p.m.	Work	
5.00 p.m.	Vespers	Church
6.00 p.m.	Meal	Refectory
6.30 p.m.	Walking	Cloister
7.30 p.m.	Bed time	Dormitory

The Sacristan's assistant wakes the monks in the dormitory. They go downstairs to the church for the service. There is a short pause at the end of prayers.

The service lasts about twenty minutes. The monks then go back to bed.

The monks are woken again.

A short service.

The service is attended by the lay brothers and abbey servants.

The choir monks, in the meantime, have breakfast of bread and ale. They are not allowed to talk during the meal. A book is read to them – perhaps the life of a saint.

Another short service.

The meeting lasts for about half an hour. Part of the founder's rule is read and monks who have broken it are given punishments. Notices are read, other business done and the day's tasks given out.

The monks walk in the cloister as they chat.

The main service of the day.

For washing only.

The meal consists of bread, vegetables, soup and wine or ale. There is more reading aloud by one of the monks. No talking is permitted.

The afternoon is spent working in the fields, gardens, cellars, scriptorium, etc.

The last service of the day.

A light meal is taken, again accompanied by readings.

In the winter, the monks stand round the fire in the warming room instead of walking.

The monks sleep until midnight when the programme starts all over again.

5 Books

Do you belong to a public library? How often do you go? Do you sometimes look for a book about your hobby? How do you find out where the book is? In most libraries, books on the same subject are together on the shelves. In Jocelyn's abbey the same kind of thing was done.

If you only have a few books in your class library, you may not need to keep them in any sort of order. How many do you need before you've simply got to arrange them properly?

At Bury St. Edmunds, the library probably had between one and two hundred volumes. They seem to have been divided into groups — Bibles, monastery rules, prayer and service books, lives of the saints, general religious books, medical books, sermons and so on. We

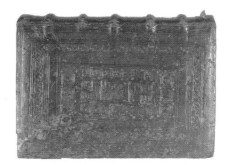

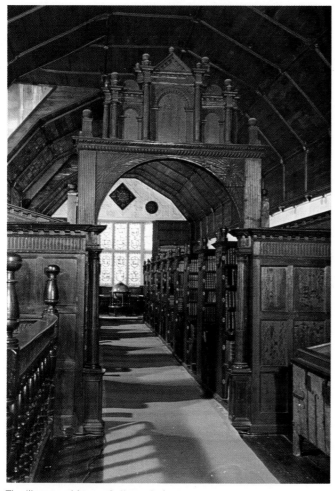

The library at Merton College, Oxford

belonging to other religious houses in England or Europe. All were handwritten, for in those days copying was the only way a book could be made. It was to be another two hundred years before printing was invented.

It is likely that the monks who were good at writing neat letters did little else. They worked at copying in a room called a scriptorium or in small rooms just off the cloister.

Monasteries like the one at Bury have been empty and silent ever since Henry VIII closed them down. Most are now in ruins. Luckily, many of the books were saved. Some went to libraries in private houses, others to colleges at Oxford and Cambridge. Some were taken by cathedrals but most ended up in the British Museum, where they still are.

don't know how they numbered all of them but each section was given a different letter of the alphabet: A for St. Augustine's books, B for Bibles, C for chronicles (histories), or S for sermons. Then all the A books were probably numbered in the order the abbey acquired them. There were over fifty by, or about, St. Augustine. It's just as well the monks had no more than two hundred books in all, or the system would have broken down.

Two hundred volumes does not sound much compared with modern libraries which stock several thousand titles but it was a large collection for the monks. Some of the books were bought or exchanged for different ones but a good many were copied from those

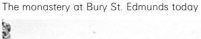

The monastery at Bury St. Edmunds today

Books

At Bury St. Edmunds, writing materials were bought from local craftsmen but other monasteries managed to produce what they needed on their own farms. Paper was dear, so they wrote on specially treated animal skins. Parchment, to give it its proper name, was made from sheep or goat skins. Vellum, which was of better quality, came from the skins of younger animals such as lambs or kids. The hides were cured with tannin. This stopped them going rotten. They were soaked in lime baths, then dried and polished with pummice stone. Tannin comes from oak trees and could also be used to make black ink.

After the skins were removed from calves, kids or lambs (*left*) they were 'cured' with tannin from oak trees. This was usually done in vats or wooden tanks (*right*). Then the skins were soaked in a lime bath to bleach and soften them and hung up to dry (*far right*).

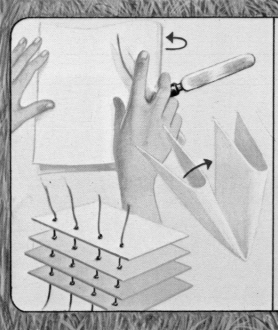

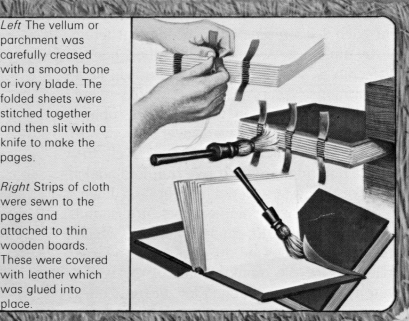

Left The vellum or parchment was carefully creased with a smooth bone or ivory blade. The folded sheets were stitched together and then slit with a knife to make the pages.

Right Strips of cloth were sewn to the pages and attached to thin wooden boards. These were covered with leather which was glued into place.

Ink was made by soaking oak-apples and mixing the liquid with flour and copper crystals. Other colours came from plants and clay.

The dry skin was stretched in a frame and polished with pumice to make it smooth and even.

6 On the Move

This is a picture from a church wall at Chaldon in Surrey. It shows what people of the Middle Ages believed about life after death. They were quite sure that good people went to Heaven and that the wicked went to Hell. But most people are neither all good nor all bad. If a man were condemned to roast in Hell for the first small sin he committed, it wouldn't be worth trying to be good any longer. He was doomed anyway.

The Church gave its followers the chance to pay for their bad deeds while they were alive. A man was allowed to go to confession and own up to what he had done wrong. The priest forgave him, provided he promised to do penance.

A man's penance, or punishment, might be to kneel in the church and say the Lord's Prayer ten times. This was for a small sin. For something more serious, he might be sent on a pilgrimage. We know that St. Edmund's tomb attracted hundreds of people every year. So did the tombs of other saints, not only in England but also abroad.

Apart from penances, pilgrims, as they were called, went to pray at tombs for quite different reasons. Some went because they were ill, to pray for good luck, or to give thanks for past favours.

How did people get about in those days? The roads were not very good. Some main roads had been made by the Romans a thousand years before and were still usable for the most part. Not everyone could journey on main roads all the time and the minor roads were no more than pathways across the countryside and through the forests.

The only reason they were there at all was because so many feet had followed the same route that the grass had been worn away. If a lot of people, animals or carts went the same way, the 'road' was wide. If not many did, it remained a path. Both were hard, uneven and dusty in hot weather and a mass of slithery mud when it rained.

Those who had to make long trips tried to arrange matters so that they went only in the summer time. Of course, it rains in the summer too but the warmer air dries the mud more quickly.

We must remember that England itself looked very different then from the way it does today. Much of it was covered with thick forests. Towns were very small and a long way apart. It was possible to plan your route in such a way that you stopped in a town each night. Travellers could nearly always stay in the guest room of a monastery. There were even a few special inns for pilgrims only. Such a place was called a 'Maison Dieu' (House of God).

Monastery food was simple and plain. There was bread, porridge, cheese, vegetables and fruit in season. Occasionally there was meat but there was nearly always fish. The guests could drink ale or wine. They might even try water if the monastery had a pure well or spring.

The monks usually made no charge for what they provided but they expected something to be put in the collecting box. A poor man could always do a little work to pay for what he had eaten.

Not that poor people travelled very much anyway, unless they were tramps, outlaws or criminals. This was because they had to go on foot. Those who could afford it rode on horseback. There were carts but they were uncomfortable and very slow. The elderly or sick could be carried in a horse litter, as Matilda had been when she escaped from Oxford Castle.

If you were lucky, you could go by boat for part of the way where your journey lay near a river or the sea. Your boat would be hauled along the river by a horse, plodding along the towpath at the water's edge. Or you might sail along the coast to where you wanted to go.

On the whole, there were not very many people on the move in medieval England.

A traveller's meal at a monastery

On the Move

7 The Story of St. Edmund

In the little museum in the Town Hall at Kings Lynn is a sheet of parchment which tells us something about how the monastery came to be built at Bury St. Edmunds. The parchment is a charter, granting to the monks of Bury the right to look after the body of St. Edmund.

Edmund had been King of East Anglia in the ninth century. His kingdom had not long been Christian but Edmund had already built churches and founded a number of small monasteries.

Unluckily for him, the Danes were still a threat to peace and order. In 869, they came down from their town of York and camped at Thetford. Edmund didn't want them in his kingdom, so he gathered his army together and marched out to meet them.

The battle was fought at Hoxne in Suffolk. Edmund's army was beaten and he was taken prisoner. The Danish leaders, Ubba and Inguar, had him brought before them.

'Accept us as your overlords,' they said, but Edmund shook his head.

'Give up your religion and become one of us,' they demanded. Edmund said he would never do so.

The Danish soldiers took Edmund into the nearby woods and tied him to a tree. The archers aimed their bows towards the king. Ubba gave an order and an arrow whistled into the tree just above Edmund's head. Again the questions were asked and again the king said no. An arrow pinned a fold of his cloak

to the tree trunk. Another grazed his arm.

When they realized that Edmund would never give up his religion, Ubba and Inguar told the archers to shoot straight at their target. The king's body slumped in its ropes. The soldiers cut it down.

The news soon spread that the king had been slain. When the Danes had gone, some of the East Anglians went to look for the body. They were shocked when they found it. Before the Danes left, they had cut off the head and hidden it in the forest.

The people beat through the undergrowth looking for the head. Suddenly some of them heard a voice crying, 'Here! Here! Here!' They followed the sounds until they came out into a clearing. They could see a wolf with the king's head between its paws. When the wolf caught sight of them, it made off into the bushes.

They brought the head back to its body and the story began to get about that the shouting had come from the head itself, that

it had told the searchers where to look. People believed the story and came to pray at Edmund's graveside to have their illnesses cured or their sins forgiven. Men left their money and their land to the church where the miracle-working body lay. The king was declared a saint and he became a hero to the Saxons in their fight against the Danes.

Sweyn Forkbeard, the leader of a later Danish army, came to the church. He was annoyed at the way that St. Edmund seemed to be a greater enemy dead than he had been alive. He decided to take away the property and lands of the church and close it down. No sooner had he given the order when he dropped to the floor dead.

His son, Canute, didn't make the same mistake. He took the hint and put monks in charge of the shrine. From these small beginnings a monastery grew.

The charter at Kings Lynn on the left gives us written proof of what Canute did all those centuries ago.

Work Section

Understand your Work

1 Monasteries
1 Where did King Stephen's son die?
2 Where is Bury St. Edmunds?
3 How did monasteries serve the community?
4 What does 'lawlessness' mean?
5 What is a nunnery?
6 What was the head of a nunnery called?
7 What were the three main rules the monks and nuns followed?
8 How were monasteries founded?
9 Look at the picture on page 22. What is Eustace holding?
10 Look at the top picture on page 23. What sorts of fish could the monks be catching?

2 Jocelyn of Brakelonde
1 In whose reign did Jocelyn live?
2 Where was Jocelyn a monk?
3 For how long did Jocelyn keep his diary?
4 What might have happened to the original book?
5 What was the name of the abbot at Bury St. Edmunds?
6 Was Jocelyn happy with the way the abbot ran the monastery?
7 What does 'defy' mean?
8 The diary no longer exists, so how do we know about it?
9 What are the main differences between the buildings inside the abbey grounds and those outside?
10 Why did the abbey have to have such high walls?

4 A Day in the Abbey
1 Who woke the monks for the midnight service?
2 What are the names of the services?
3 What was the longest period of sleep the choir monks could have?
4 What happened during breakfast?
5 What happened in the scriptorium?
6 What was the dining room called?
7 What was the 'founder's rule'?
8 What is a cloister?
9 On pages 28 and 29 you can see pictures of the places where the monks sleep, wash and eat. How are they different from the places where you do these things?
10 In the dining room scene, what is the monk likely to be reading from?

5 Books
1 In what way is a modern library similar to the one at Bury St. Edmunds?
2 How many books did the monks at Bury St. Edmunds have?
3 What sort of books were they?
4 How were the books arranged?
5 How did the monks acquire their books?
6 How many printed books did the monks have?
7 Who closed down the monastery at Bury St. Edmunds?
8 What happened to the books when the monastery was closed?
9 How is the modern library different from the one at Merton College?
10 How are the medieval books shown in the pictures different from the ones you use?

6 On the Move
1 What did the people in the Middle Ages believe about life after death?
2 How could a man pay for his bad deeds while he was alive?
3 What is a 'penance'?
4 What is a 'pilgrimage'?
5 What were medieval roads like?
6 What is a 'Maison Dieu'?
7 In which season of the year was it best to travel?
8 Why didn't poor people travel very much?
9 Who are the figures shown in the mural on page 34? What are they doing?
10 Look at the picture on page 36 and 37. What are the main differences between travel in summer and travel in winter? How many different forms of transport can you list?

7 The Story of St. Edmund
1 What is a charter?
2 The Danes came to East Anglia in A.D. 896. Where did they camp?
3 Over which kingdom did Edmund rule?
4 Who were the Danish leaders?
5 How was Edmund killed?
6 Who tried to confiscate the property of the church?
7 Who was this man's son?
8 Where is the charter now?
9 Describe what is happening in the picture on page 38.
10 In which language is the charter at Kings Lynn written?

Use your Imagination

1 Why do you think that only the brightest or the richest children were educated by the monks?
2 The monks looked after sick people. Today, hospital patients are looked after by doctors and nurses. How are modern patients better cared for than those in the Middle Ages? Think about transport, equipment, medicine, comfort and hygiene.
3 Monks and nuns had to give away all their 'wordly possessions'. What are wordly possessions? Would you be happy to give up yours?
4 What makes Jocelyn's diary so valuable? Why is it much more valuable than one you might keep today?
5 Study pages 24 to 29. How was a monastery like a village? In which ways was it different?
6 Look at the picture on pages 26 and 27. An expert could guess the date of the picture by looking at the children's clothes. We could not do the same by looking at the monks' clothes. Why not?
7 Describe the objects each of the monks is holding and say what you think his job is.
8 Why do places like monasteries, schools and army barracks have to keep timetables? What might happen if they did not have them?
9 Somebody joining a monastery must have found it hard to get used to the strict discipline. What would you have found hardest about the life?
10 How do you know where to find a book in a modern library? The system the monks used was simpler because they had fewer books. Why would the monks' system not work today?
11 The painter of the picture at Chaldon church had to use his imagination to show hell. Why? Try painting your own picture of hell. Make it as horrible as you can.
12 Imagine that you are one of the characters in the picture on pages 36 and 37. Write an account of your journey. Say where and why you were going, how long it took and where you stayed.
13 Today people travel far more than they did in medieval times. Why? There are few monasteries today. Where do travellers stay?
14 Why do you think that people believed that a dead Saint could help them cure their illnesses?
15 Look at the pictures shown on pages 32 and 33. Do you think the same monk would have done all the jobs shown? Give reasons for your answers.

Further Work

1 Monasteries taught children and looked after the sick. On page 22 you can read about some other services the monks provided. Find out who provides these services today.
2 Monks didn't charge for their services. Help they gave was known as 'charity'. What modern charities can you think of? Are they similar to the monks' form of charity? How is money raised for charities in modern times?
3 Many early monasteries started as hermitages. What is a hermit? Find out all you can about these early monasteries. Can you remain silent as long as the monks did? Start with a short period of time in class while you are carrying out other tasks. What particular difficulties do you notice?
4 Find out how paper is made today. Why was it dearer than parchment in medieval times but cheaper than parchment now?
5 How long do you think it would take you to copy a book by hand? What would be the best way to produce twelve hand-written copies of the same book if you had several people to help you?
6 Why do you think Sweyn was known as 'Forkbeard'? How many other kings can you think of who had nicknames?
7 There is a famous story about King Canute. Can you find out what it is?
8 Why did people in the Middle Ages believe that it was important to confess their sins?
9 Find out why the medieval English monasteries are mostly in ruins.
10 Find out how long it would have taken you to get from your own home to the centre of London in medieval times.
11 Try making a book in the way shown on pages 32 and 33. You can use paper instead of parchment.
12 Find your nearest medieval monastery and try to visit it. You will be able to get a guide book which contains a plan of the monastery. Find the church, the refectory, the cloister, the chapter house, the lavatory and the dormitory. You might like to sketch the ruins of these buildings as they are today.

Chapter Three   The Crusades

1 Peter the Hermit

Pilgrims visited foreign shrines, as well as the tombs of English saints. Those of St. James in Spain and Saints Peter and Paul in Rome were popular. A few English pilgrims went on beyond Rome right down to the south of Italy. From there they sailed across the Mediterranean to the Holy Land. Sometimes they broke their journey at either Crete or Cyprus.

They were making the longest and most important pilgrimage of all. They were going to pray at the places where Jesus had lived and died. For several centuries, the Holy Land had been occupied by Arab peoples. They were followers of Mohammed, but they did not stop Christians going to Jerusalem or Bethlehem.

Then, at about the same time as the Battle of Hastings, a new race of people appeared in the Holy Land. They were the Turks. They too were Muslims like the Arabs but they were much fiercer and crueller. They captured Jerusalem in 1076 and from then on, Christian pilgrims could not go where they

Some crusader routes

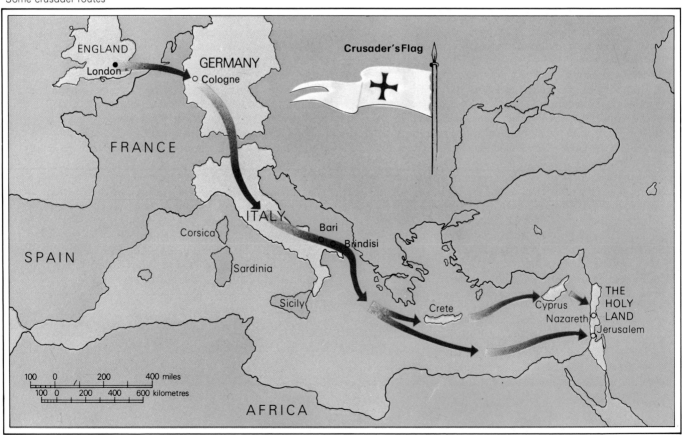

liked. The Turks turned them back, arrested them, threw them into prison and tortured them.

The Emperor at his capital city, Constantinople, sent a message to the Pope, telling him of the danger and asking for help. It was not just because pilgrims were having a hard time. The Emperor had seen how fast the Turks had conquered some of his own lands and he was afraid that Constantinople would be next on their list.

The Pope realized that if the Emperor was right, there would be nothing to stop the Turks sweeping across Europe. He urged all Christians to forget their own wars.

'It is a Christian's duty,' he said, 'to drive the unbelievers out of the Holy Land and free the holy places from their soldiers.' He said these things during a sermon he preached in 1095.

Among those who heard him was a French priest. The people called him Peter the Hermit. He made up his mind to bring the Pope's message to as many Christians as he could.

Let's pretend we are living in a small town on the banks of the River Rhine. What might we have seen?

The news has got around that Peter is expected this very afternoon. The people have gathered in the town square. Most of the craftsmen have shut up their businesses and are standing about in groups of two or three. Even the children know that there is something different about today.

Some apprentices have been larking about a little way down the road. One of them shouts, 'He's coming!' The rest stop their game and make way for Peter. He is riding on a donkey. He comes to a halt and gets down. He looks about him and sees a stone cross at one side of the square. He walks towards it and then faces the townspeople.

They all look at him. He is tall and sunburnt. Both his hair and beard are long and

uncombed. He wears a rough, one-piece garment with wide sleeves. It reaches to his ankles and would be even longer without the rope he wears round his waist to hitch it up. He fingers the crucifix hanging on his chest and begins to speak. His voice is very low to start with but it rises higher as he talks.

He tells the people what is happening in the Holy Land. He makes them angry at what the Turks are doing. He makes some of them weep. He makes them all proud to be Christians.

'The infidels must be driven out,' he shouts. Many of them join in the shouting.

'Take me with you,' cries one.

'I'll help you fight the Turks!' yells another.

On the next page, we'll see what happened to them.

2 Wars of the Cross

'Crusade' means 'war of the cross'. It comes from the same Latin word as 'crucifix' and 'cross' itself. It was a crusade that Peter the Hermit meant to wage against the Turks.

His army was not much more than a mob but they set out from Cologne on the Rhine full of enthusiasm. They left in April, 1096, making their way along the valley of the River Danube.

When they got to Hungary, many of them did stupid things. They thought they were already among the Turks just because they could not understand the local language. Fights broke out and men were killed on both sides. What was left of Peter's army reached Constantinople by July.

Peter thought they ought to wait until the proper soldiers arrived. Armoured knights would be coming to do battle with the Turks but they wouldn't arrive in Constantinople for several months. It wasn't so easy for the knights. They couldn't just pick up a pitchfork and set out for the East as Peter's men had done.

The Emperor did not want Peter's rabble to stay in his capital too long for fear they might cause more trouble. The men were so eager to fight they wouldn't listen to Peter. The Emperor sent them off in ships to the Holy Land. Of course, they were no match for

Peter and his followers were no match for the Saracen army.

the well trained Turks, or Saracens, as the crusaders called them. Peter's men were so badly beaten that few of them lived through the battle.

It wasn't until the following year that the knights got to Constantinople. They were much better organized and led, and there were a lot of them. Although they were sincere in wanting to do their Christian duty, there was another reason why some of them had come.

Many were the younger sons of nobles. A younger son knew that his elder brother would have the family lands when father died. Lands were not shared out between the children. Those who were left out jumped at the chance of setting up their own estates somewhere abroad.

After two years of fighting, the crusaders finally captured Jerusalem. Thinking that this was the end of the problem, a large part of the army packed up and went home. Those who wanted to stay set up a Christian kingdom with a Norman knight as their ruler. Several of the barons built castles on their new lands and tried to live the kind of life they had known back in Europe.

The Arabs and Turks did not like being ruled by Christians and did all they could to get rid of them. They were within easy reach of help for there were more Turkish soldiers not far away. There were not so many Christians and if they wanted help, it could take months to reach them.

The Turks attacked again and again and a second crusade had to be launched against them. It failed, and in 1187, the Turks recaptured Jerusalem. In spite of six more crusades during the next century, the crusaders never won it back again. In fact, the Turks were not forced out of the city until the First World War. This was over six hundred years later, in 1917, and in the lifetime of some people who are still alive now.

3 New Ideas from the East

In spite of themselves, some of the Christians had to admire the way the Muslims lived. The crusaders copied these ways and took them back to Europe. They brought back the carpets and wall hangings of the East and put them in their castles. A few improved their table manners. They stopped using their fingers and began to use forks as the Arabs did. They learned to use spices, such as pepper, with their food. This was to become very important later.

As trade improved between East and West, other new ideas appeared in Europe. Not all of them had been thought up by Arabs or Turks. Quite often they had just been passed on from places like India and China. They included better ways of sailing, telling the time and working out sums.

Our own numbers are based on those the Arabs copied from India. It was much easier for merchants to keep their accounts with the new figures. All the same, the new system didn't catch on straightaway. The old Roman letters hung on for centuries and are not completely dead even now. Do we not still write 'Henry VIII' rather than 'Henry 8'?

jewellery

rock crystal

ivory

glass

enamel

rice

perfume

astrolabe

mirror
cloves

ginger

nutmeg

porcelain

almonds

Arabic numerals

wall hangings

cloth embroidered
with gold

satins, silks, velvets and dyes

dates

raisins

gar

green figs

carpets

black pepper

fork

4 A Knight and his Family

As the years went by, the living standards of the rich slowly got better. The poor went on in the same old way. They had no fashions and few improvements in their homes.

Let's look at what a knight's life was like in the early thirteenth century. We'll just call him Sir John. He held his lands from the Abbot of Valle Crucis. He was not a great

rewarded by hearing a voice joining in the chorus. He had found his lord.

By this time, the king's subjects in England had raised most of the ransom, which in today's money might be about two or three million pounds. Richard was released and returned to England.

John thought it wiser to slip away to France. Richard had to raise an army and take it across the Channel to defend his lands in Normandy. He spent the last five years of his life abroad. He was killed by an arrow while besieging a French castle called Chaluz.

Richard was known as 'Coeur de Lion' which means 'Lion Heart'. He would have understood the first title better than the second, for although born in England, he spoke French and thought of himself as French. All the same. he was one of the bravest warrior kings we have ever had.

above Leopold of Austria

below Richard killed at Chaluz

7 Armour and Siege Weapons

The fighting man on horseback was an important kind of soldier during the early Middle Ages. His armour had changed little since the end of the Roman empire. Roman legionaries had worn strips of metal over their shoulders and round their chests. The tribes which had overrun their empire had used a different arrangement.

Barbarian warriors had worn coats of leather covered all over with little metal rings, discs or plates. They were sewn in place. The Normans wore something like this when they invaded England.

Linking the rings together makes chain mail. It was more expensive than the old leather coat style, for it took more metal and needed a great deal of skill to make. Crusaders had to wear a light linen coat over it to

Roman

Barbarian

Crusader

Detail of chain mail links

protect themselves from the heat in the lands where they were fighting. The coat was white with a red cross on it. There was a slit at the front and back to make horse riding easier.

Another drawback to any kind of metal armour, especially chain mail, was the fact that it rusted if it wasn't looked after. A Roman could wipe and dry his plate armour if it got wet. It wasn't so easy to do the same thing to a suit of chain mail with its thousands of little links. There was no stainless steel in those days so the knight's squire would have to protect the links by painting them with varnish.

Christian armies spent most of their time besieging castles and towns rather than fighting pitched battles against the Saracens. The Romans had worked out ways of attacking the defenders of a fort. They were very good at it, and the methods had not altered greatly in the centuries that had passed since their time.

The difficulty was the wall which formed the outer works of most castles. The attackers had to get inside somehow. There were three ways to to this. They could go over the wall, under it, or knock it down. Here are some of the 'engines' and methods the attackers used.

Undermining

Battering

Siege tower

Catapult

8 A Siege

9 Magna Carta

Richard Lion Heart died in 1199 and his younger brother, John, became king. The early histories tell us that he wasn't a very pleasant person. He had been spoiled as a child and it's hard to find something nice to say about him. His eating habits were disgusting. He often stuffed himself with food until he couldn't move, or drank himself senseless. He was just as uncivilized in other matters, leaving a trail of trickery and broken promises behind him.

John had a nephew named Arthur. Philip of France thought that John was treating the boy badly. War broke out between the two kings. John took Arthur prisoner. His barons asked him to set the boy free. John promised them that he would but he had Arthur murdered instead. Philip won the war and took most of John's French land away from him.

John then quarrelled with the Pope who promptly closed all the churches in England. This was a disaster for Englishmen. Most of them thought they were bound for Hell as a result. The Pope also said that John was not a fit person to be a king and asked Philip to invade England. John gave in and agreed to pay money to the Pope.

Biding his time, John collected an army and invaded France himself. He was badly beaten. This time his barons had had quite enough of him. Defeats and the heavy taxes needed to pay for the wars were too much for them.

They drew up a list of their complaints against the king and threatened to attack his castles and estates. John agreed to meet them at Runnymede in an open field alongside the Thames between Windsor and Staines. The field has changed very little since those days. There are few buildings in sight, so it's easy to stand there and imagine what the meeting must have been like.

It is a June morning in the year 1215. There has been a light mist but it has gone now. The sun shines from a clear blue sky, picking out the bright colours of the tents which have been put up. There is a carved wooden throne for the king to sit on, if and when he should come.

Some of the rebels are wondering if the king means to keep his appointment. Quite a few of the barons who had promised to come have not turned up. They know that John will never forgive those who have put this shame on him. The group at Runnymede is uneasy. Are they risking their lives by trying to force the king to rule according to the law?

There is a stir in the crowd. In the direction of Windsor some horsemen can be seen picking their way along the river bank. The king's party stops near the tents. Grooms hold the horses as they dismount.

The king sits on the throne. The barons and churchmen have drawn up a list of their complaints. It is on a sheet of parchment. One of them unrolls it and begins to read. There is a short pause when he has finished. John beckons a servant forward. Wax is heated over a flame and the parchment is spread out on a small table in front of the throne.

The wax is poured out and John presses

his Great Seal into it before it can harden. The meeting is over. The king leaves to ride back to Windsor Castle. The barons and churchmen will now have to have the Great Charter, or Magna Carta, as they call it in Latin, written out properly. The experts will get together and put it into the kind of words that lawyers understand.

The king has had to agree, among other things, not to interfere with the Church and not to imprison nor sentence a man without trial. He must give back the forest land he had enclosed without permission and defend the ancient rights of towns and cities. He must allow a baron to be tried by men of his own class, and not raise taxes without consent.

John had no intention of keeping these promises and even got the Pope to say that the Magna Carta was not lawful. When the barons realized that this was the case, civil war broke out. John did not live long enough to see what happened. He died after greedily eating a huge meal of peaches and cider. Some people muttered that he had been poisoned but no one knows for sure.

Magna Carta with John's Seal

Work Section

Understand your Work

1 Peter the Hermit
1 What is a shrine? Which ones were popular?
2 How did pilgrims get from England to the Holy Land?
3 Of which religion were the Turks?
4 What did the Turks do to Christian pilgrims?
5 Where was the Emperor's capital city?
6 Who preached a sermon in 1095?
7 Where is the River Rhine?
8 What is Peter wearing?
9 What was Peter's nationality?
10 How far is it from England to the Holy Land?

2 Wars of the Cross
1 What does 'crusade' mean?
2 Which river did Peter's men follow from Cologne?
3 What happened in Hungary?
4 How long did it take Peter's army to reach Constantinople?
5 Why didn't the armoured knights reach Constantinople as quickly as Peter's army?
6 Why didn't the Emperor want Peter's men to stay in Constantinople?
7 What happened to Peter's men?
8 What happened in 1187?
9 Look at the picture on page 44. With what are Peter's men armed?
10 Look at the crusader on page 45. Describe his weapons and his armour.

4–5 A Knight and his Family/Family Affairs
1 Did the living standards of the poor improve?
2 Where was the Abbey of Valle Crucis?
3 Why is it too dangerous to have the front door at ground level in Sir John's manor house?
4 What materials were used for windows before people started using glass?
5 What does Lady Isobel have to do?
6 What does the family drink and where do the drinks come from?
7 How could Sir John raise money for his campaign in the Holy Land?
8 What might the town gain by giving money to Sir John?
9 Look at the picture on pages 48, 49. What are the white birds to the left of the main entrance of the house? Why were such birds kept?
10 Look at the picture on pages 50 and 51. Can you see how the rooms were lit? What else might have been used?

6 Richard the Lion Heart
1 How long did Richard the Lion Heart spend in England? How long did his queen spend?
2 Why did Richard spend so little time in England?
3 What sort of war was Richard fighting in 1192?
4 How did Richard return home?
5 Who captured Richard?
6 Was Richard killed during a crusade?
7 What was Richard's native language?
8 Where is Chaluz?
9 Is Richard buried in Westminster Abbey?
10 Describe what is happening in the bottom picture on page 53.

7 Armour and Siege Weapons
1 How was the armour of the Romans different from that of their barbarian enemies?
2 What sort of armour did the Normans wear?
3 Why was chain mail expensive?
4 Why did crusaders wear light white linen coats?
5 Why was Roman armour easier to clean than chain mail?
6 Did Christian armies spend most of their time fighting pitched battles with the Saracens?
7 Did the crusaders have to work out methods of besieging castles for themselves?
8 What three ways are there of getting inside a castle?
9 Why are the arms and legs of two of the soldiers on page 54 left unprotected?
10 Why does the battering ram on page 55 have a solid roof?

9 Magna Carta
1 How were John and Richard related?
2 What tells us that John was an unpleasant sort of character?
3 What was the name of John's nephew? What happened to him?
4 What action did the Pope take against King John?
5 In which year was Magna Carta sealed?
6 What does Magna Carta mean?
7 To what did King John have to agree?
8 How did John die?
9 What is hanging at the bottom of the charter?
10 Describe what is happening in the picture on page 59.

Use your Imagination

1 What do you think Peter the Hermit actually said to the people of the Rhineland? You might try to make up a speech for him. Get one or two people to make their speeches to the class. Does it matter how the speech is read or said? Are some people better at making speeches than others?

2 Why do you think the Pope was particularly keen to keep the Turks out of Europe?

3 Some of Peter's men behaved very badly when they got to Hungary. Why do you think some people do stupid things when a) they are in large groups; b) they are away from home?

4 If the leaders of a country and its people are of different religions, are there likely to be problems? What sort of problems may there be?

5 Why, do you think, the Roman system of numbering did not die out as soon as the new method was introduced?

6 Look at the picture on pages 46 and 47. How many of the things in the picture could you find in your own home? As well as new ideas, the crusaders brought back many new words from the East. Why do you think this happened?

7 Why do you think that the living standards of the rich improved whilst those of the poor did not?

8 One of Sir John's servants has to make sure that the manor house has enough food for several months. If you had this job, how would you go about it? Make a shopping list for your own family for three months. You will have to be careful about the sort of things you buy because some foods won't keep for more than a few days and there certainly aren't any freezers or refrigerators.

9 Imagine what your own kitchen would be like without any of its modern inventions. You wouldn't even have gas or electricity. Describe how you would set about making a simple meal.

10 Sir John wants to go to the crusades. Lady Isobel wants him to stay at home. Make up an argument between them using points from the text. You could make it serious or funny.

11 What do you think the ordinary people of England thought about a king who hardly ever visited them?

12 There is no doubt that Richard enjoyed fighting wars. Few people today enjoy war. What has changed?

13 Imagine that you were a knight's squire. Describe your duties.

14 Imagine that you are a soldier at the siege shown on pages 56 and 57. Describe what is happening.

15 King John had some serious quarrels with the Pope. The historians who wrote about King John during his lifetime were monks living in monasteries. Why do you suppose they were so keen to emphasize the bad parts of John's character?

16 Why, do you think, did John go to Runnymede if he had no intention of keeping the promises he made?

Further Work

1 Draw a picture of a crusader in armour. You may be able to find a crusader's tomb in a local church, if it is old enough. There are many memorials to crusaders on brass plates in churches. You might like to make a brass rubbing of one.

2 Find out how long the crusades lasted.

3 Design and draw a fortified manor house of your own.

4 You can see from Peter the Hermit's disastrous expedition that it is unwise to go to war unprepared. Sir John is going on the crusade with fifteen of his men. Describe the preparations he will have to make and list the equipment he should take. Be warned – it could be a very long list!

5 Find some pictures and descriptions of a siege in Roman times. Find pictures of the siege equipment that the Romans are using. Are there any great differences between Roman equipment and that used in medieval times?

6 Find out when English kings stopped using French as their first language.

7 Find out all you can about the 'children's crusade'. Write your own account of what happened.

8 Crusaders brought back many new ideas from the East. In modern times the British ruled an empire in India. Can you think of any practices, objects or words that have been brought from India?

9 Find out when and how your own town got its charter.

10 Find and retell the famous story of how King John lost the crown jewels.

11 What can you find out about a legendary outlaw who was supposed to have lived during the reigns of Richard I and King John?

Chapter Four   Years of Change

1 Four Kings

HENRY III

EDWARD I

EDWARD I WAS ONE OF ENGLAND'S MOST WARLIKE KINGS. HE CAME TO THE THRONE IN 1272. THE PEOPLE OF WALES REFUSED TO ACCEPT ENGLISH RULE. EDWARD DEFEATED THEM IN 1281 AND KILLED THEIR LEADER, LLEWELLYN, IN BATTLE.

TO KEEP THE WELSH IN ORDER, EDWARD BUILT STRONG NEW CASTLES ALONG THE COAST OF NORTH WALES.

EDWARD II

EDWARD II CAME TO THE THRONE IN 1307. HE WAS A GOOD HORSEMAN AND SKILFUL IN THE USE OF WEAPONS, BUT HE WAS MORE INTERESTED IN ENJOYING HIMSELF THAN FIGHTING BATTLES. HE SPENT FORTUNES ON HIS FRIENDS, FASHIONS AND ENTERTAINMENTS. EDWARD ALSO ENJOYED MAKING FUN OF OF HIS BARONS WHOM HE CONSIDERED DULL-WITTED AND UNCOUTH.

EDWARD III

EDWARD III WAS ANOTHER WARLIKE KING. HE SPENT MUCH OF HIS LIFE FIGHTING THE FRENCH. ONE OF HIS MOST FAMOUS VICTORIES WAS AT THE BATTLE OF CRECY, WHERE HIS SON 'THE BLACK PRINCE,' WON HIS SPURS. THE FRENCH LOST ABOUT 15,000 MEN. THE ENGLISH LOST 100 MEN.

WHEN EDWARD CAPTURED THE TOWN OF CALAIS FROM THE FRENCH, HE SEIZED SIX OF THE CHIEF CITIZENS. THE KING WAS ANGRY THAT THE TOWN HAD HELD OUT SO LONG. THE MEN WOULD HAVE BEEN EXECUTED IF THE ENGLISH QUEEN HAD NOT PLEADED FOR THEIR LIVES.

HENRY III BECAME KING IN 1216 WHEN HE WAS ONLY NINE. HE ALLOWED THE POPE TO TAX THE COUNTRY VERY HEAVILY. THE KING QUARRELLED WITH HIS BARONS AND CIVIL WAR BROKE OUT. HENRY WAS CAPTURED AT THE BATTLE OF LEWES IN 1264.

ONE OF THE MOST IMPORTANT EVENTS OF HENRY'S REIGN WAS THE OPENING OF WESTMINSTER ABBEY. IT HAD TAKEN TWO HUNDRED YEARS TO BUILD.

SIMON DE MONTFORT WAS THE LEADER OF THE REBEL BARONS. HE FORCED THE KING TO PAY MORE ATTENTION TO A COUNCIL OF ADVISERS. THE COUNCIL CAME TO BE KNOWN AS THE 'PARLIAMENT'. SIMON WAS EVENTUALLY KILLED AT THE BATTLE OF EVESHAM BY HENRY'S ELDEST SON, EDWARD.

EDWARD OFFERED THE WELSH PEOPLE A RULER, WHO SPOKE 'NO WORD OF ENGLISH'. HE HAD IN MIND HIS BABY SON WHO COULDN'T SPEAK ANY LANGUAGE. EVER SINCE, THE HEIR TO THE ENGLISH THRONE HAS BEEN CALLED THE PRINCE OF WALES.

EDWARD THEN DECIDED TO CONQUER THE SCOTS. HE CAPTURED THE STONE OF DESTINY ON WHICH SCOTTISH KINGS WERE CROWNED, AND BROUGHT IT TO LONDON. IT IS STILL SET UNDER THE ENGLISH THRONE.

THE SCOTS WERE CRUSHED AT THE BATTLE OF FALKIRK IN 1298. THEIR LEADER, WILLIAM WALLACE, WAS EVENTUALLY CAPTURED, HUNG AND QUARTERED.

ROBERT BRUCE, THE SCOTTISH KING, DEFEATED AN ENGLISH ARMY LED BY EDWARD, AT THE BATTLE OF BANNOCKBURN IN 1314. BEFORE THE REAL FIGHTING BEGAN ROBERT WAS ATTACKED BY ONE OF THE ENGLISH KNIGHTS, SIR HENRY DE BOHUN. KING ROBERT AVOIDED SIR HENRY'S LANCE AND SPLIT THE ENGLISHMAN'S SKULL WITH A BATTLE-AXE.

IN 1327 KING EDWARD II WAS CAPTURED BY A GROUP OF HIS BARONS. THEY KEPT HIM IN A DISUSED WELL FOR WEEKS AT BERKELEY CASTLE, AND EVENTUALLY MURDERED HIM. WHEN EDWARD'S SON WAS MADE KING HE EXECUTED HIS FATHER'S MURDERERS.

EDWARD III DIED IN 1377. TOWARDS THE END OF HIS REIGN THE FRENCH WENT ON THE ATTACK. THEY CAPTURED THE ISLE OF WIGHT FOR A TIME AND EVEN MARCHED INTO KENT.

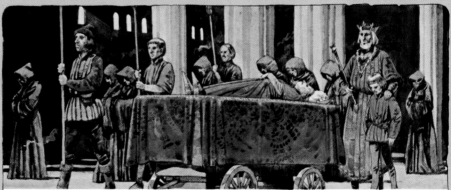

EDWARD III'S SON, THE BLACK PRINCE, DIED BEFORE HIM. THIS WAS A GREAT BLOW TO THE KING, FROM WHICH HE NEVER RECOVERED. THE BLACK PRINCE IS BURIED IN CANTERBURY CATHEDRAL. THE NEXT KING WAS EDWARD III'S GRANDSON, RICHARD II, WHO WAS ONLY TWELVE WHEN HE WAS CROWNED.

2 The Wool Trade

One of the highest officials in the land is the Lord Chancellor. This is a picture of him in the House of Lords. Why, do you think, is he sitting on that cushion instead of a chair?

If you could look at England in the 1300s you might be surprised at what you saw. There were not as many towns as there are now and those that did exist were much smaller. The countryside was not divided by hedges into thousands of little fields and there was a lot of land that no one seemed to use or want.

Normally, three huge fields were spread out around each village. Sheep were everywhere. There were millions of them – far more sheep than people, in fact. If you thought that a lot of mutton was eaten in those days, you would be wrong. Sheep were not kept for their meat. Mutton was eaten, but the wool was more important. Most people made their own clothes. The wool for the cloth came from their own sheep. Even the spinning and the weaving were done at home.

Far more wool was produced than could be used in England, so the extra fleeces were sold overseas. English cloth was well made but rather coarse. If you wanted really good clothes, you had to get them from Europe. The strange thing was that, although the finest materials were woven in France or Italy, the weavers often used English wool.

All this means that there was a lot of travelling and trading to be done. Wool was sheared from the sheep and taken to the nearest town to be sold. It could be piled on to carts or slung over the backs of pack-animals. Whenever possible, it was loaded on to boats.

Foreign merchants travelled to England from France, Flanders and Italy to buy up the English wool clip and sell it in their own countries. After a while, English merchants began to take the wool overseas themselves and England soon came to depend on the money made from this trade. To remind important people where the country's wealth came from, cushions stuffed with fleece were made for them. That is why there is still a wool sack for the Chancellor to sit on in the House of Lords. One of the reasons why Edward III started the Hundred Years War was a French threat to the wool trade.

Let us follow an imaginary journey that an English merchant is making. John de Barnes has been on the road for several days now. He is riding a horse in company with two other travellers he has met on Watling Street. It is better for them to journey together. It is not safe to be out on one's own. There are too many cut-throats, outlaws and thieves about.

The travellers have been staying in monasteries or inns each night and this is their last day together. Tonight they will lodge at Stoneleigh Abbey in the Midlands. Tomorrow John will say goodbye to his com-

panions who are going on. He will meet the abbot in the morning and then go out to the sheep-folds.

To make sure he gets the first pick of the best wool, he needs to make the monastery an offer even before the sheep are sheared. Last year, he arrived too late and found the fleeces had already been sold to merchants from Flanders.

This year he is in time. The abbot is pleased to get his money and the shearing begins. It is done with hand-clippers. The fleeces are crammed into canvas bags which are then sewn up and taken by packhorse to the coast. John leaves his agents and servants to look after the packhorses and rides eastward to the port of Kings Lynn.

He is anxious until the wool arrives. The bags are weighed by the customs officers and stamped with his mark. They are loaded on to a ship as soon as John has paid the duty. The ship will sail to Calais in France. There John will put up his wool for sale. The buyers will take it to Ghent or Bruges and sell it to the Flemish spinners and weavers.

The profit John makes in Calais will be lent to a friend of his there, who will buy lengths of luxury cloth. These will be brought back to England in John's ship. When the rich materials are sold, John will have his loan returned plus a second lot of profits.

3 The Ship

4 A House in London

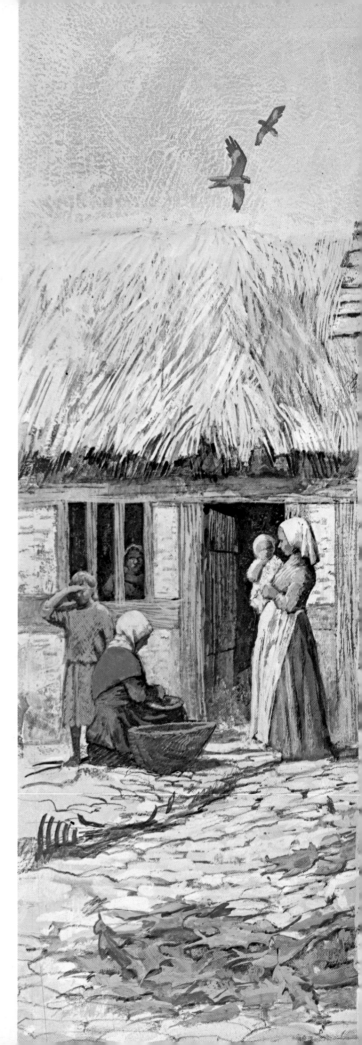

We catch up with John de Barnes on the road to London. He tells us that he is looking forward to seeing his family again.

'I've been away several weeks now, and I'll be glad to get home. The ship landed me at Dover. I rode here to Canterbury where I met this group of pilgrims. They have been to pray at the tomb of St. Thomas à Becket. Some of them have decided to stay here in Kent because there is a plague in London.'

'What sort of plague?'

'Well, every summer there is disease from which people die but the pilgrims say that this year it's much worse than usual. I hope they are exaggerating but I'm worried all the same. My wife and family are back in London. I pray they are all right.'

5 The Black Death

Black rat   Plague flea

The October sun is warm on his back as John rides over London Bridge and clatters on to the cobble-stones of the city. His horse picks its way past the heaps of rubbish which dot the streets.

He is relieved to see his wife at the door when he gets home.

'Don't worry, John', she says. 'The children are fine but several people have been taken ill in this very street and some have died. It's a new kind of plague, and it's all over London. Poor Mistress Bates has lost her husband and both her children.'

John finds out that his neighbours are beginning to call this new plague 'the Black Death'. This is because of what happens to those who are unfortunate enough to catch it. It starts with a sore throat and a runny nose, followed by really bad headaches and a high fever. Then dark splotches appear on the skin, rather like large bruises. Lumps swell up at the tops of the arms and legs. Within a few days, the patient dies.

There are doctors of a kind but they know neither the cause nor the cure. Today, doctors call the disease bubonic plague and they are sure that it was spread by rats and fleas. There are plenty of these in medieval England. It is quite likely that John's wealth has spared him and his family. His stone house does not have so many rats as the wooden, thatched houses of his neighbours.

John loses no time in moving his family

to a house he has in the country. He is lucky that the village is not visited by the Black Death. Because living conditions in the countryside are not so unhealthy as those in towns, many people have followed John's example and moved out. Some of them, without knowing it, have taken the plague with them.

We don't know how many people suffered but some experts say that as many as one out of every three English people died. Fields were not farmed and weeds grew everywhere. Stalls in market places were empty and ships stayed in port. Prices went up, for there were not enough people left to grow or make all the things that were wanted. Here and there whole villages were deserted as the people died or moved away.

The Black Death is thought to have been

above All that remains today of Tusmore, a village deserted during the Black Death

brought here from the East in 1348. It came back three times in the 1360s and continued to return every few years for the next three centuries.

6 The Peasants' Revolt

John Ball

Edward III died in 1377. The next king was his grandson, Richard II. He was only ten years old. Before he was fifteen, a serious rebellion broke out. It happened in 1381 and is known as the Peasants' Revolt.

There were several reasons for the rebellion. To begin with, the Black Death had killed so many people that the pattern of everyday life was upset. There were not enough people to work the fields but lords still expected their work to be done.

Parliament passed laws which tried to keep wages and prices down but they were not successful. On top of everything, the wars with France dragged on, costing more and more money. The peasants were taxed and taxed again. The last straw came when the government decided to raise a poll-tax. The word 'poll' means 'head'.

There were wandering priests who went round the countryside preaching that all men should be equal. One of these preachers was a man named John Ball. Let's listen to one of his sermons.

'My friends,' he says, 'your lives are miserable and poor. Things are wrong with England and they will not be put right unless you do something about them. Poor man hates rich man; rich man sets his face against poor man. Nothing will be better until the good things are shared out fairly.

'The rich man wears beautiful clothes and eats fine foods from silver plates. You wear coarse cloth and eat dry bread from a wooden platter. He drinks wine; you have nothing but water. He sleeps in a bed between linen sheets; you have to put up with mouldy straw on the ground.

'What makes him think he is better than you? We are all the children of Adam and Eve. How did he get rich at our expense?'

The villagers shout their agreement. John Ball tells them that they must be ready to act when the time comes.

The poll-tax did not bring in as much as the king's advisers expected. A lot of people dodged payment, so collectors were sent round. In some villages they were beaten up and dumped in the duck pond. The people armed themselves with pitchforks, knives and sickles.

At Brentwood in Essex, the officials sent to deal with the trouble were mobbed by the peasants. A few were killed by the angry countrymen. Their heads were cut off, stuck on long poles and paraded around the nearby parishes. Now there was no going back. The men of Brentwood sent messengers all over Essex to tell everyone that the time had come for change. Some rowed across the Thames to get help from the people of Kent.

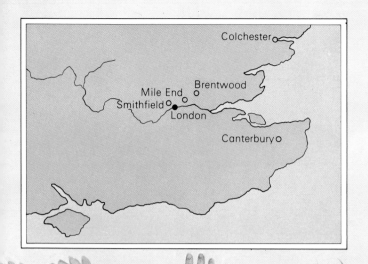

Groups of peasants began to move off westward from both Kent and Essex. They intended to march to London. The Kentish rebels chose a man named Wat Tyler to be their general. Later he became the leader of all the peasants.

Other bands of rebels captured the main towns in the two counties, including Colchester and Canterbury. In the last-named city, they smashed their way into the cathedral and the palace looking for the archbishop. They believed him to be responsible for their miserable condition.

The rebels got the idea that the boy king, Richard, did not know what was going on. They thought that as soon as he was told everything would get better.

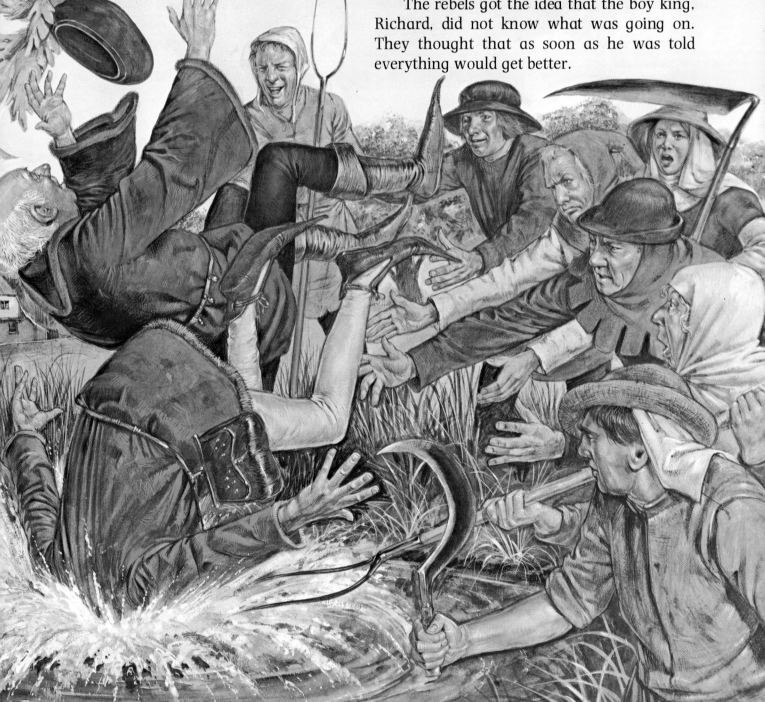

The Peasants' Revolt

On their way up to London, the groups of peasants broke into manor houses. They took food when they could find it, although Wat Tyler and John Ball insisted that they paid for what they ate. More often, they searched the houses for the parchment rolls which set out the details of the unpaid work the peasants had to do for the lord. They carried the piles of parchment outside and burned them.

The ragged army reached London and sympathizers inside the walls opened the gates to them. They destroyed the homes of the hated lawyers and officials and even hanged some of them. The rebels refused to go home until they had talked to King Richard II.

Finally, the mob met the king at Mile End. Richard promised to do what they wanted and set his lawyers to work to draw up the agreements. At Smithfield they met again.

Then things went wrong. Tyler seemed to threaten the king. The lord mayor struck at the peasant leader with his sword. He was pulled from his horse and hacked to death.

When Richard saw that Tyler was dead, he rode towards the mob, shouting to them that he would be their leader. By promising them a better life, he managed to get them to go home.

Later, soldiers were sent to round up the rebels and hang some of them. But the landowners and lords had learned a lesson. Slowly, serfdom began to die out although it took a long time to disappear completely.

7 A King's Banquet

The boy king, Richard II, had a troubled reign in other ways. Eventually, he was forced to hand over his crown to his cousin, Henry. The new king, Henry IV, shut Richard up in Pontefract Castle, where he was later murdered. Henry left the Tower of London where he had been staying and was crowned in Westminster Abbey.

After the coronation, everyone went in procession to Westminster Hall where the banquet was to be held. The tables were covered with gold and silver dishes and the new king sat down surrounded by his courtiers, the two archbishops, seventeen bishops, all his lords and knights, together with the Lord Mayor of London and his aldermen.

The king's champion rode into the hall in full armour and offered to fight against anyone who dared to say that Henry IV was not the rightful king. There were no takers.

A small army of servants brought in the food. You can see what they ate from the menu on this page.

The decorations mentioned did not just come at the end of a course. They were put on or with any dish that seemed to need them. They were made of pastry, jelly or sugar, moulded into shapes, figures, or animals. Often they were gilded. Coats of arms, religious stories and hunting scenes in coloured sugar were popular.

No attempt was made to group the dishes in any sort of order. It was normal to serve a sweet in between two dishes of roast meat and the whole lot was washed down with wines from many lands. How different from the bread, cheese and porridge of the poor. No wonder there was a Peasants' Revolt.

First Course
Brawn in pepper and spice sauce · Royal pudding · Boar's head · Fat chicken
Herons · Pheasants · Cygnets · Date and prune custard
Sturgeon and pike · *Decorations*

Second Course
Venison in boiled wheat and milk · Jelly · Stuffed sucking pig · Peacocks
Roast bitterns · Glazed chicken · Cranes · Roast venison · Rabbits
Fruit tarts · Cold brawn · Date pudding · *Decorations*

Third Course
Beef in wine and almond sauce · Preserved quinces · Roast egret · Curlews
Pine nuts in honey and ginger · Partridges · Quails · Snipe · Small birds
Rissoles glazed with egg yolks · Rabbits · Sliced brawn · Iced eggs
Fritters · Cheesecakes · Small rolls · *Decorations*

8 In the Kitchen

Here is a recipe, in the original old English, fr[...]

Storion in brothe.—Take fayre Freysshe Storgeoun, an choppe it in fayre water; þanne take it fro þe fyre, an strayne þe brothe þorw a straynoure in-to a potte, an pyke clene þe Fysshe, an caste þer to powder Pepir, Clowes, Maces, Canel; & þanne take fayre Brede, and stepe it in þe same lycowre, & caste þer-to, an let boyle to-gederys, & caste þen Safroun þer-to, Gyngere, an Salt, & Vynegre, & þanne serue it forth ynne.

On the right is a modern translation of the recipe.

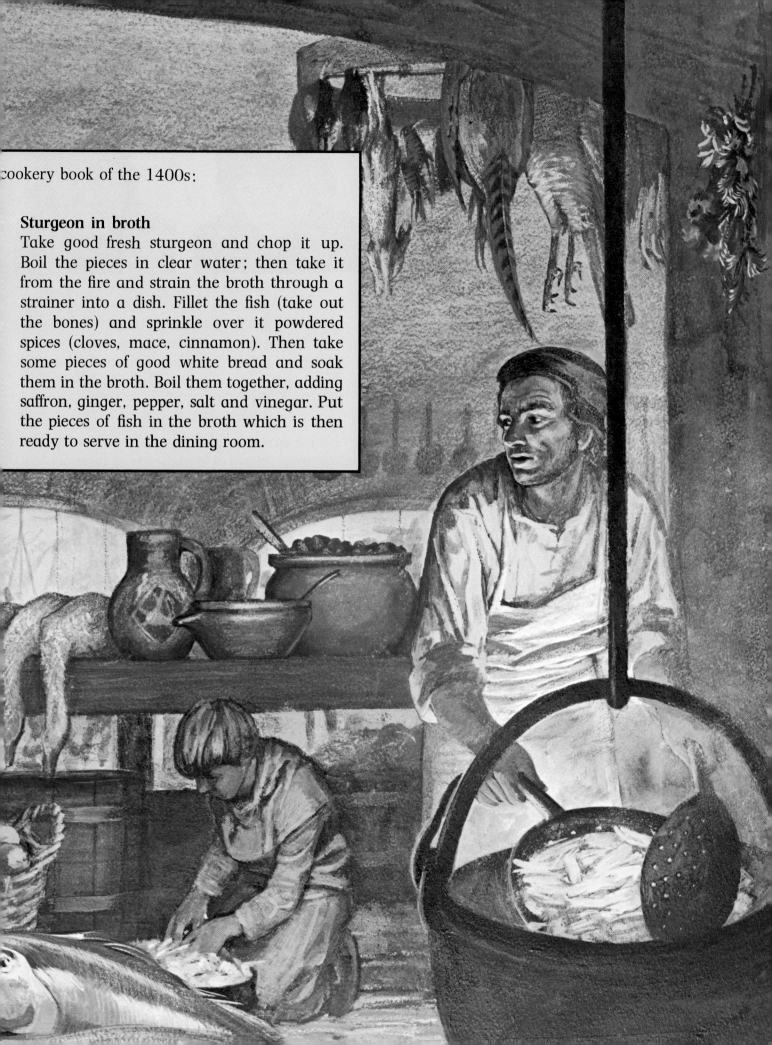

cookery book of the 1400s:

Sturgeon in broth
Take good fresh sturgeon and chop it up.
Boil the pieces in clear water; then take it
from the fire and strain the broth through a
strainer into a dish. Fillet the fish (take out
the bones) and sprinkle over it powdered
spices (cloves, mace, cinnamon). Then take
some pieces of good white bread and soak
them in the broth. Boil them together, adding
saffron, ginger, pepper, salt and vinegar. Put
the pieces of fish in the broth which is then
ready to serve in the dining room.

9 William of Wykeham

This is the story of William, a boy who grew up to be one of the most important men in all the land. He was born at Wickham, a little place about half-way between Southampton and Portsmouth. His father's name was John Long.

It seems likely that 'Long' was a nickname. In earlier times, few people had more than one name. Villages were small and it was enough to be known as 'John', 'Peter', 'Mary' or 'Alice'. As the numbers of people grew, this method no longer worked.

When you came to a large village looking for John, you would be asked which one you wanted.

'There are seven Johns here', you might be told. 'Do you mean John the son of William, John the son of Wat, John the thatcher, John the blacksmith, John the tailor, John who lives near the forest or John the tall man?'

In time, these ways of telling people apart would turn into Williamson, Watson, Thatcher, Smith, Tailor, Forest and Long. Our boy William ought to have been called William Johnson but he became so famous that his title as a grown-up was William of Wykeham. Wykeham was how Wickham was spelt in those days.

He was a bright boy and was sent to the grammar school at Winchester to be educated. This school was mainly for the sons of Winchester citizens and was not the same as the one King Alfred had founded 400 years earlier.

As a young man, William's first job was as secretary to the constable of Winchester Castle, Robert of Popham. He soon obtained

Building New College in Oxford

Winchester College has been a school for over 600 years.

a position with King Edward III. He worked well and was promoted. In 1359 he was put in charge of castle and house repairs along the south-east coast. The Hundred Years' War was being fought and French raids had damaged our defences.

In 1366, he was made Bishop of Winchester and the following year, Chancellor of England. He used a lot of the money he had made to found both a college and a school. He bought land for the buildings to stand on and more land to bring in an income. In this way, both school and college would be able to carry on after his death.

One of the reasons for his interest in education was his desire to replace the huge number of priests which the Black Death had carried off. He wanted his school, 'Seinte Marie College of Wynchestre', to send its best pupils to his new college at Oxford. The boys were to be the sons of parents who could not afford the money otherwise.

Wykehamists have been going on to New College ever since – a period of nearly 600 years.

New College today

10 St. Erkenwald

At the same time that William of Wykeham's school and college were being founded, a famous London landmark was being rebuilt. Everyone knows what St. Paul's Cathedral looks like now but the one we see today is only 300 years old. It replaced the one burnt down in the Great Fire of 1666.

The first church on the site was probably a Saxon one, also burnt down. The Norman cathedral was started about 1250 and it had already taken over a century to finish. Just as Londoners were looking forward to its opening, a story in verse was written, retelling one of the legends of St. Erkenwald who had been a popular Bishop of London as far back as the year 675.

WORKMEN ARE DIGGING OUT THE FOUNDATIONS FOR THE NEW SAXON CHURCH WHEN THEY FIND A WONDERFUL OLD TOMB.

HE STANDS OVER THE COFFIN AND ASKS THE DEAD MAN WHO HE IS.

THE PEOPLE ARE AMAZED WHEN THE CORPSE OPENS HIS EYES AND ANSWERS. HE SAYS HE IS AN HONEST JUDGE AND HAS BEEN DEAD FOR 1,700 YEARS. HE SITS UP. HE SAYS THAT HIS PEOPLE HONOURED HIM WITH A FINE TOMB. AND THAT GOD HAS KEPT HIS BODY FRESH BECAUSE HE WAS A JUST MAN. ERKENWALD ASKS HIM WHY HE DID NOT GO TO HEAVEN IF HE WAS A GOOD MAN. THE OTHER REPLIES THAT HE DIED BEFORE CHRIST WAS BORN SO HE COULD BE NEITHER BAPTISED NOR SAVED.

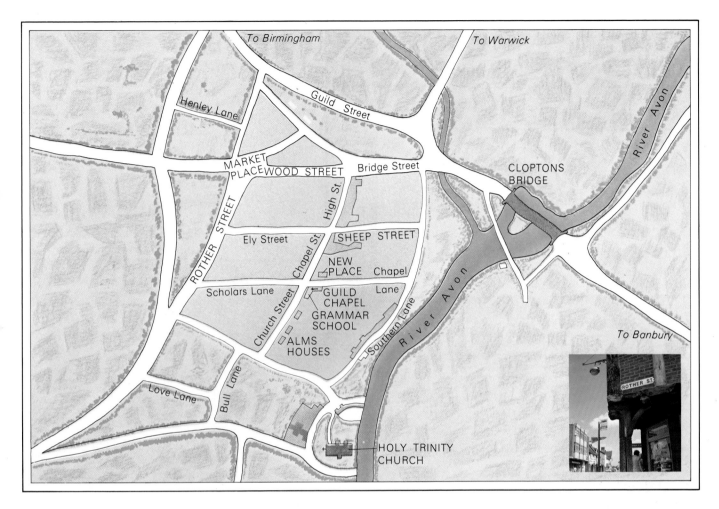

dwellers who bought from the peasants. All the same, it was a rare house or workshop that didn't have space for a cow in the back yard and perhaps even a few fruit trees in the garden.

Even though you could walk all round medieval Stratford in about twenty minutes, the houses were not crammed together. The gardens, orchards and open spaces saw to that.

Some of the country folk came into town on market days to sell their sheep, cattle, cheese, corn and vegetables. The money was spent on what they couldn't make or produce themselves, including ironware, barrels, leatherwork and some clothing.

It's not really surprising to find so many different kinds of things on sale in so small a town. Travel was not easy. Roads were bad and journeys were measured in days rather than hours. It could take a week to get to London by the fastest transport you could afford. Poor people hardly went anywhere very much. As walking was their only way of getting about they probably never journeyed more than a day's walk from where they were born all their lives.

Even the streets of the town were bad. There were no pavements and only a few cobble-stones here and there. Apart from that, Stratford had everything you could want — food, drink, shelter, clothing, entertainment, religion. The town had a fine stone church and a guild chapel, a school, four fairs a year, occasional visits from a band of actors and a weekly market. What more could anyone ask?

2 Medieval Tradesmen

Cooper

The cooper needs as much wood as the wheelwright. It was discovered that wine and other drinks keep better in wooden containers than in clay pots. Early craftsmen may have tried to scoop out the inside of a large block of wood. This takes a long time and wastes a lot of wood. A better way is to cut a number of staves and fit them together with iron hoops. The barrel will be used to hold beer or wine.

Charcoal-burner

The woodcutters haul the logs to a clearing in the forest. The charcoal-burners chop the logs into small pieces. These are piled into a large heap and covered with turf. The men drop burning pieces of charcoal into the pile of wood which smoulders slowly for several days. When the wood turns black it has become charcoal. It is sold to those who want a smokeless fuel with no impurities. Rich men buy it for use in their kitchens and iron smelters burn it in their furnaces.

Potter

The potter sends his assistants to dig clay from the pit near the river. They bring it back in a cart and pummel and knead it on a flat bench. The potter takes a lump of the clay and puts it on his wheel. He uses his feet to turn the wheel and his hands to shape the jug. Pottery in the Middle Ages is rough but not cheap. Some is glazed in green or combed in brown and yellow before it is fired in a kiln.

Wheelwright

The wheelwright also gets timber from the woodcutters. He needs three different types of wood — elm, ash and oak. The elm is used for the hub of the wheel which is huge and weighs several pounds. It has to be made carefully as it must be absolutely round and the eight holes for the spokes need to be cut very accurately. The spokes are made from ash. They are shaped and fitted into the hub sockets. The felloes are the pieces of oak which form the wheel rim. They fit on to the spokes and are fixed in place when the wheelwright nails strips of iron across the joints.

Medieval Tradesmen

Innkeeper

In the Middle Ages many peasants brew their own beer. Some make better beer than their neighbours so they produce more than they need and sell the excess. A few become innkeepers and provide drink and food for those who can afford it. At an inn travellers can get a bed for the night, a stable for their horses and, perhaps, a barn for their servants.

Moneyer

The moneyer and his helpers make coins. Poor people don't use money. They barter or exchange goods directly. This means that most coins are made of gold and silver for the use of the rich. The moneyer beats out the ingots of metal into sheets of the same thickness as the finished coins. He then cuts out the discs with a large pair of sharp shears. The disc is called a blank. The blank is set on top of a metal die and another die is placed over the top of it. The moneyer then gives the top die a sharp blow with his hammer. If it has been struck just right, the two dies will make the pattern on both sides of the coin at once.

Weaver

Just as most peasants brew their own beer, so most of them make their own cloth. For those who can't or don't have the time the weaver goes to work. He winds his threads of wool in a special way on his warping board to stop them tangling. Then he puts threads, one at a time, through the little eyes in the heddles and fastens them in bunches to the front beam of his loom. By pressing down a pedal with his foot the weaver can raise one lot of threads. This makes a space through which the shuttle thread is passed.

Miller

The peasant farmers all take their corn to the mill to be ground. The mill is leased out by the lord of the manor to the miller who is one of the wealthy men of the district. His mill stands alongside the river and the machinery is driven by a water wheel. The miller raises a sluice gate and the water pours past the mill and turns the wheel. The wheel makes the two millstones revolve against each other. The corn trickles down between the stones and is ground to flour.

3 The Cordwainer's Apprentice

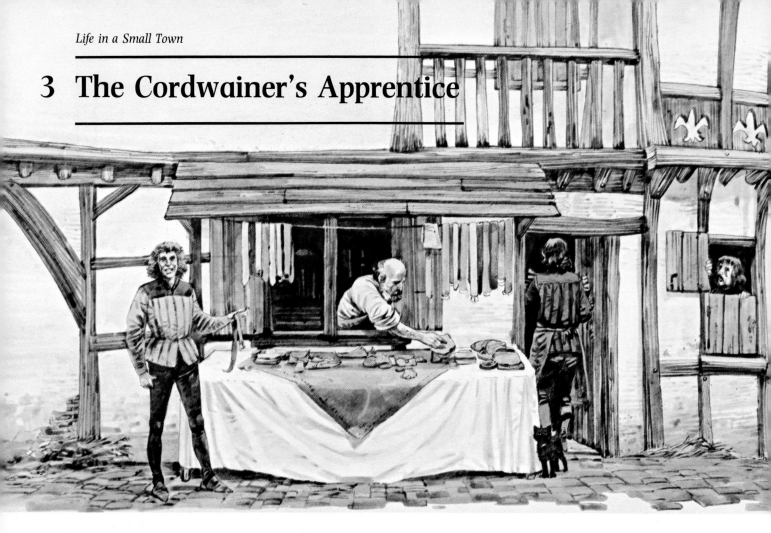

Towns in the Middle Ages were not large by our standards. If there were two or three thousand people in a town, it was considered to be a big one. Most people still earned their living by farming but town dwellers, on the whole, did not.

We have already seen that there were men in the Middle Ages who specialized in making just one thing. Most crafts of this kind were not open to everyone. You could not become a wheelwright, for example, without serving an apprenticeship. This meant that you would have to spend several years learning the job before you could open your own business.

Even today, apprenticeships have to be served for some careers. In the Middle Ages, this was true for almost any trade that needed the slightest bit of skill. To find out what an apprentice's life was like we shall ask the cordwainer's boy some questions. His name is Ralph.

'*What exactly does a cordwainer do?*'

'He is a worker in leather, but he is not a common cobbler or shoemaker. He does make shoes but rather fine ones. His main trade is in anything made of goatskin.' Ralph shows us some belts, purses and bags. They are made from what we would call suede leather. We still don't know why a leather worker should be called a cordwainer. Ralph will explain.

'The best goat-leather comes from Cordova in Spain. We call it Cordovan or Cordwain. I had to learn about these things when I first joined the trade. Luckily for me, my master means to teach me properly. Some masters don't do this and treat their boys as though they were cheap servants. You see, we don't get paid for what we do. On the contrary, my father has had to pay the cordwainer to teach me.'

'When did you become an apprentice?'

'Most boys start their apprenticeship when they are fourteen and it usually lasts seven years. By the time I'm twenty-one, I will know how to work with all kinds of leather, which kinds of stitching and thread to use and which types of buckles, clasps and ornaments to buy. There's a lot to learn about buying and selling and it isn't easy.'

As Ralph is speaking, one of the workmen starts to take in the goods on display and put up the shutters of the shop. It's only midday but it seems that all the workshops are shutting. Ralph explains what is happening.

'Today is a half-holiday for the apprentices,' he says. 'This afternoon we are going to play football.'

'Are you in the team?'

'Everybody's in the team!' he says in a surprised voice. 'You can watch if you like but, if I were you, I'd do it from an upstairs window.'

Later that afternoon, we take his advice. No one, apart from the apprentices, seems to be in the street.

The match starts near the middle of the market square. The ball is a small barrel of ale. There appear to be hundreds of players on each side. There are no rules as far as we can see and no referee. Linesmen are not needed, for the 'pitch' is wherever the 'ball' goes. Boys push the little barrel with their feet. They don't kick it for fear of breaking their toes. Every now and then, someone picks it up and tries to run. He doesn't get far before he is bowled over. The game surges all over the town and we can now see why all the shops close for the day. A mass of bodies is crammed into the narrow street where we were talking to Ralph. We realize that if the goods had still been on show they would have been scattered and trodden on. The whole stall would have probably ended up in pieces.

Some of the players are giving up. One has twisted his ankle on the cobble-stones and another has blood running down his forehead. The rest carry on. The game ends when the first goal is scored. The goals are at the end of Bridge Street in one direction and at the crossroads in the other. It's not often that the goal is scored and the game normally ends when it's too dark to see what is going on.

4 The Guild System

Miles Collins

While we are waiting for the football match to finish, we ask Miles Collins, Ralph's master, about the guilds in the town.

'I expect you've heard about the Mercers' Guild? They are men who buy and sell cloth. Men who work at a craft all belong to their own special guilds. Just think of the things you need which you either can't produce yourself or perhaps you just don't have the time to make.

'For example, there are guilds for each type of metal worker. Blacksmiths turn out iron tools and implements while other kinds of smith work with lead, tin, copper, silver or gold. Most are concerned with everyday objects such as pipes, pots and pans but the last two, silversmiths and goldsmiths, make jewellery and fine table-ware.

'Then there are the various leather workers like myself. Tanners deal with the coarser hides and tawers with the finer ones, such as kid. There are boot-makers, cobblers and glovers and there are the men who make saddles and harnesses for horses. Even the stitching of cow hides into bottles and jugs has its own craftsmen.

'There's almost as big a group involved in woodwork of some kind. Separate guilds deal with furniture makers, plain carpenters,

Coats of arms of four of London's main guilds

sawyers, wheelwrights, cartwrights and so on. I could go on for quite a while.'

'*What exactly is a guild? It sounds like a sort of club.*'

'It is a club, in a way. All the members look after each other. If a man has the tools of his trade stolen, the guild will replace them. If a man falls on hard times or becomes ill, his guild will take care of him. It will see that his wife doesn't starve should he die. His fellow guildsmen will even pay for his son's apprenticeship.'

'*Where does the money come from to do all this?*'

'Oh, each member puts in a small sum. It adds up to quite a large amount when there are lots of members. Only masters have to pay the subscription.'

'*How did you become a master?*'

'I started as an apprentice, like young Ralph. I served my seven years and then I became a journeyman. That's a sort of skilled workman. Each apprentice has to pass an examination. He answers questions from a panel of masters and has to show them an example of his work. After a few years, if he works hard enough and saves his wages as I did, he may have enough money to start his own business.'

'*Everyone seems to work very hard.*'

'Oh it's not all work. You've seen the apprentices having their game of football. Of course, the masters don't join in but there are plenty of other pastimes we help with. Life is quite hard for most people so we seize any chance we get to have some merrymaking – a feast, a procession or a play. Our guild is rehearsing a play at the moment. Perhaps you would like to come and watch?'

Examples of guild craftsmanship

5 The Play

Miles is obviously keen on drama and knows a lot about the subject. He tells us something of its history.

'Guild members are good Christians,' he begins. 'You may have seen the guild chapel in Chapel Lane. We paid for that. You won't be surprised to hear that our play is religious too. The idea for a play started years ago in the days when hardly anyone could read or write. To help people understand stories from a Bible they couldn't read, some churches had paintings and carvings arranged around the inside of the church itself. Obviously, these were scenes from Bible stories. Then monks began to act out the scenes. They just did the actions with a storyteller to explain what was happening. Perhaps each playlet was put on near the picture or carving of the scene so that the audience would have to move round to follow the stories. After a while, the actors began to speak the lines and make up material which was not in the Bible.

'Audiences enjoyed the comedy which had crept in and more people crowded into the church to watch. So many came that before long, there wasn't enough room for them all inside. The actors moved outside to the churchyard and eventually to important points around the town.

'Each guild acts out its own part of the story and moves on to the next stage as soon as it is over. The guild performs several times in different places. Those watching can see the whole set, or cycle of playlets, by staying where they are.'

At last we come to the yard where the rehearsal is in progress. There is hardly any make-up and few special clothes or stage properties for the actors. Everyone seems to know their words. We watch what is going on.

The stage is known as the pageant and is almost head-high to an adult. It stands on four large wheels so that it can be pulled through the streets to the places where the play will be performed. Miles strolls over to have a word with the actors on the stage. Then Ralph comes into the yard. We ask him if he is in the play.

'Well, I was last year but not this. I said that I thought the Christmas play should be more like the one they do at Coventry. They do the same as we do for the birth of Jesus but they have this funny piece to start with about a thief called Mak, and the shepherds. Mak steals a sheep and hides it in the cradle at his house. The shepherds notice one of their flock has gone and call on Mak. They think the sheep in the cradle is a baby and Mak shouts at them for disturbing it and its mother. They apologize and leave but a minute after they have gone, one of them remembers that they haven't given the baby a present. So they decide to go back. One of the shepherds goes to the cradle with a sixpenny piece and discovers that the baby is really the missing sheep! They threaten to have Mak hanged but after a while, they let him off with their own punishment. Mak is put on a sheet of canvas and tossed in the air several times.'

Ralph is smiling as he says this until he sees the blank look on our faces. 'Well,' he says defensively, 'it doesn't sound so funny as it is when you see it.'

The Play

6 Hugh Clopton

Back in the thirteenth century, during the reign of Henry III, a man named Robert became the owner of an estate and manor house at Clopton. Clopton House still stands in parkland about a mile to the north of Stratford upon Avon in Warwickshire. From then, the owner called himself Robert de Clopton ('de' is French for 'of').

About two centuries later, the 'de' had been dropped and there was born at the House a boy who was known simply as Hugh Clopton. We don't know the exact year this happened but we do know that he went to London when he was still quite a young lad.

He was probably apprenticed to a high-class cloth merchant. By the 1470s, he had become very wealthy. In October 1485, he was elected alderman of the Dowgate ward. It was an honour to be chosen to sit on the Corporation of the City of London. It was fine to have the power to make rules for your fellow citizens to live by but it meant that Hugh had even less time to spend in his beloved Stratford.

This was a pity, for he had built a fine house in Chapel Street, Stratford, in 1483. It was timber-framed like most houses of its day but the gaps between the wooden struts were not filled with wattle and daub (plastered basketwork) but with good red bricks.

The Romans had often used bricks when they were here but after they left, the secret of making them had been lost, or else they had just gone out of fashion. It was to be a thousand years before they were included in buildings again. Hugh Clopton's house, New Place, as it was called, must have been one

Alderman's costume

of the first houses in Stratford to have bricks.

Only eight years later, Hugh Clopton became Lord Mayor of London and was knighted. He may also have been elected to Parliament at about this time. In the short period he was able to spend at Stratford, he tried to make improvements to the town which would please the people who lived there.

He started with the guild chapel almost opposite New Place. He gave it a steeple and new glass windows. He arranged to have the inside decorated with paintings, some of which can still be seen.

One thing the visitor can hardly help noticing is the fine stone bridge over the River Avon. This too was the gift of Sir Hugh. The old wooden bridge had become rickety and unsafe. Sir Hugh paid workmen to drive closely-packed wooden piles in circles where the foundations of the arches were to go.

The men cleared away the mud and sand from inside the wooden pile rings and dug down to make holes for the foundations. Stone masons shaped and fitted the blocks together and finally it was done. Its fourteen arches were so well built that the bridge stands to this day.

The building of Hugh Clopton's bridge

above Clopton's bridge today

below The Guild Chapel in Stratford

The story of Sir Hugh Clopton is rather like that of Dick Whittington. Both were country boys who became mercers in London. Both were knighted and both were chosen as Lord Mayor. Both became rich and left money for the poor. There must have been many like them.

Another poor boy from the country made good in London and came back to pass his last few years in his native town. Towards the end of the sixteenth century, he bought New Place from the descendants of Sir Hugh Clopton. His name was William Shakespeare.

7 New Place

Clopton's fine house was pulled down in 1759. All we have left of it are a few sketches and the gardens that William Shakespeare set out when he moved in. Here is a picture of what the house must have looked like in Clopton's day. Walls have been cut away so you can see what is going on inside.

8 Family Chapels and Chantries

This is the inscription carved on Shakespeare's tomb in Stratford parish church. It was natural in a religious age for men to feel that they stood less chance of going to Heaven if their remains were scattered or destroyed.

Another way of making sure of eternal life was to have masses, or services, said for your soul after your death. The easiest way to make certain they were said was to leave land in your will, with instructions that the rent from it was to be paid to priests to pray for you.

Such an instruction set up what was known as a 'chantry' and because they cost

money, they were not for the poor. Peasants didn't have land, so they got a simple funeral service and that was that. The rich man's land was intended to provide the priest's wages for ever. When the priest himself died or resigned, the money was there to appoint someone else.

Wages were not the only expense. All the robes and vessels had to be bought, as did the ornaments and candles. The most expensive item on the list was the building of the chapel, or at least altering the church in which it was to be put.

The Clopton chapel in Holy Trinity Church, Stratford, is a good example of a family chapel. Although Sir Hugh died in London and is buried there, his money paid for a tomb altar in memory of him. Many other members of the Clopton family have tombs or memorials there.

Holy Trinity Church in Stratford

The Clopton chapel

The first chantry chapels were set up in the thirteenth century. By the fifteenth century, there was scarcely a parish church

that didn't have a family chapel, or at least a chantry priest or two.

Some of the richer chantries also set aside money for charities. These might be schools, colleges, homes for orphans or almshouses for the aged poor. Those not rich enough to found colleges might arrange a chantry for a few weeks or months, or if that was too dear, then they could leave some money to buy candles for the parish church.

If a man were a member of a guild he might be lucky enough to share in a guild chantry paid for by all the members. In London alone, during the early 1500s, there were more than seventy such guild chantries.

A question you may be asking is, 'What happened to these chantries — why don't you hear of them nowadays?' You can of course visit any of the churches which have family chapels. Holy Trinity at Stratford isn't the only example — there are plenty of others.

The reason why you won't have heard of a priest being paid to do nothing else apart from praying for just one person's soul is simply that they don't exist any more. Henry VIII and his son Edward VI passed laws taking over all the land whose rent paid the salaries of the priests. As a result, the chantries had come to an end by the middle 1550s.

9 King Richard III

This is the Tower of London. It is a grim-looking fortress. Many stories, some true, some merely legends, have given it a sinister reputation. A great many people have been imprisoned here. A number of them were executed, others were never heard of again. In 1674 the skeletons of two boys were discovered under the floor at the foot of the staircase.

Here are two pictures of Richard III. One is a portrait painted during his lifetime. The other is a famous actor playing the part of Richard in a Shakespeare play.

When King Edward IV died in 1483, his eldest son should have become king but the boy was only 12 years old. Richard was the prince's uncle. He promised to keep the lad safe until he was old enough to rule.

Richard was also appointed to run the country in the meantime. Instead of protecting the prince he put him and his brother in the Tower of London. Then he declared that neither of the two princes in the Tower could be the next king. Weeks later, he had himself crowned as King Richard III.

In Shakespeare's play about him, he is made to seem the worst villain that ever lived. There is certainly a strong chance that the skeletons mentioned above are those of the two princes and that their uncle had them murdered.

Those of Richard's subjects who didn't like the way he did things whispered among themselves that perhaps the exiled Earl of Richmond would make a better king. After all, he was a descendant of Edward III. Some of them were so disgusted with Richard that they went over to join the earl in France. In 1485, Henry, Earl of Richmond, landed with an army in Wales. He moved north and then turned inland. Richard III met him at Market Bosworth, about 12 miles west of Leicester. Henry had 5,000 soldiers but Richard had almost 15,000 – not that he could rely on all of them. In particular, Lord Stanley, who was in command of a large number of men, waited to see which way the battle would go.

Richard was anxious to fight against Henry man-to-man and tried to get at him. After a while Stanley gave the order and his men started to fight; unluckily for the king, they joined in on Henry's side. Stanley's soldiers surrounded Richard and hacked him to death.

The crown which he had been wearing fell off and rolled into a thorn bush. Lord Stanley picked it up and put it on Henry's head. Then he knelt before him and motioned to his followers to do the same.

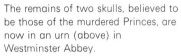

The remains of two skulls, believed to be those of the murdered Princes, are now in an urn (above) in Westminster Abbey.

Henry Tudor, Earl of Richmond, had become Henry VII. The new age which was about to begin is known as the Tudor period from his family name.

Work Section

Understand your Work

1 A Market Town
1 About how many people were there in England in the Middle Ages?
2 What is a market town?
3 What is meant by 'surplus'?
4 What ways are there of crossing a river?
5 How were houses made in the fourteenth and fifteenth centuries?
6 Why didn't craftsmen have time to grow all their own food?
7 Was medieval Stratford a cramped and crowded place?
8 What sort of things were sold in the market?
9 Look at the picture at the top of page 104 and describe the stall.
10 Look at the map on page 105. Find a church, Sheep Street, Rother Street, the market square, the bridge and the Guild Chapel.

3 The Cordwainer's Apprentice
1 How did most people earn their living in the Middle Ages?
2 What is an 'apprenticeship'?
3 What is a 'cordwainer'?
4 Do all masters treat their boys fairly?
5 How much did apprentices get paid?
6 What sort of things will Ralph learn?
7 How is the medieval game of football different from our own?
8 Why do all the tradesmen shut up their shops before the game of football starts?
9 The cordwainer paid for the cobbles outside his shop. Can you think why they were necessary?
10 Of what are the buildings in the pictures on pages 110 and 111 made?

4 The Guild System
1 What was a 'mercer'?
2 What was the difference between a cordwainer and a bootmaker?
3 What is a 'sawyer'?
4 What is a 'guild'?
5 What sort of services did a guild provide for its members?
6 What is a 'subscription'?
7 Who examines the apprentices?
8 Why do you think the masters didn't join in the game of of football?
9 What is happening in the picture at the bottom of the right-hand column of page 112?
10 What do the pictures at the top of page 113 show?

5 The Play
1 Who paid for the Guild Chapel in Chapel Lane?
2 What are the guild plays about?
3 Why did guilds start performing plays?
4 Why did it become impossible to hold the plays in the church?
5 How was it possible to see a whole cycle of plays by standing at one point in the town?
6 How high is the pageant?
7 Who is Mak?
8 Do you think the play about Mak and the Shepherds sounds funny?
9 Can you find out which is being played in the picture on page 114?
10 In the picture on page 115 what is Miles wearing on his belt?

6 Hugh Clopton
1 How did Hugh get the name Clopton?
2 How did Hugh Clopton make his money?
3 Why was New Place different from the other houses in Stratford?
4 In which year did Hugh become Lord Mayor of London?
5 What did Hugh do for the Guild Chapel in Stratford?
6 What did Hugh do about Stratford's old wooden bridge?
7 What was a mercer?
8 Who bought New Place from Hugh's descendants?
9 Describe how a bridge was built in medieval times.
10 Describe what the alderman is wearing on page 118.

8 Family Chapels and Chantries
1 What is a mass?
2 Why did some people have masses said for them after their deaths?
3 Why were chantries not for the poor?
4 What sort of things were provided in a chantry?
5 Where is the Clopton Chapel?
6 How many guild chantries were there in London in the early 1500s?
7 What other charities were there in the fifteenth century?
8 Which two kings put an end to chantries?
9 Describe the scene on page 122.
10 Where is the chapel in the picture on page 123?

9 King Richard III
1 Why does the Tower of London have a grim reputation?
2 Why didn't Edward IV's son become king?
3 Who wrote a play about Richard III?

4 Who was the Earl of Richmond?
5 Where is Market Bosworth?
6 Who had the largest army at the battle of Bosworth Field?
7 What part did Lord Stanley play in the battle?
8 Which king followed Richard III?
9 Look at the picture at the bottom of page 125. What is the king holding?
10 What heraldic devices can you see in the picture?

15 The historians who were working during the reign of King Henry VII painted a very black picture of King Richard III. Some modern historians believe that Richard was not as evil a man as the Tudor historians suggest. Why might it have been difficult for a Tudor historian to have spoken well of Richard III?
16 Do you think it's likely that the skeletons of the two boys discovered in 1674 were those of Richard's two nephews?

Use your Imagination

1 Imagine you are paying a visit to Stratford in the Middle Ages. Describe how you get there, what you see and where you stay.
2 Choose one of the craftsmen on pages 106 to 109. Describe what his job is, how he does it and why it is important.
3 Imagine you are Ralph, a cordwainer's apprentice. Write a letter to your parents saying what you are learning and how you are enjoying your apprenticeship.
4 Why do you think the guild system has almost died out?
5 Who, do you think, went to the schools provided by the guilds? Who do you think didn't?
6 What are the most interesting features in your own town or village? What would you like to show a visitor?
7 Why do you think coins minted in the Middle Ages are much more valuable today than when they were first made?
8 What sorts of foods and objects can you buy today that you could have bought in medieval Stratford?
9 Imagine you are Ralph and that you have been watching a football match in which your friends have been playing. Describe the game to a friend.
10 How are plays today different from plays in medieval times?
11 In what ways is the story of Hugh Clopton like the story of Dick Whittington?
12 Imagine you have been staying with Hugh Clopton at New Place. Describe to a friend what the house is like.
13 Why were people so worried about their souls in medieval times?
14 If the chantries had not been abolished during the reigns of Henry VIII and Edward VI, do you think they would have survived until today? Give reasons for your answer.

Further Work

1 Find out who founded Eton College and King's College Cambridge and how he died.
2 Find out which trades still have apprenticeships.
3 Visit your nearest old town. List all the old buildings in the town centre and try to discover their age. You could photograph or sketch the old buildings and write a short history of each one. It would be best to start with the oldest and work forward.
4 In the Middle Ages travellers often had to change their money when they visited another town. Nowadays we only do this when we go abroad. What currencies are used in other countries? How long a list can you make?
5 Find out how medieval towns were supplied with water.
6 Find out who saw to it that the law was not broken in a medieval town.
7 Find out how leather goods, such as shoes and gloves, are made today. How have things changed since the Middle Ages?
8 Find a modern version of the play about Mak and the Shepherds. It is called the Second Shepherd's Play from the Wakefield pageants in the Towneley cycle. You could try and perform some of it.
9 Find out what happened to New Place.
10 Are there any street names in your own town or village which suggest that the streets existed in medieval times?
11 The Tower of London has a grim reputation. Thousands of people visit it every year. Why do you think people are attracted to places with a horrific reputation? Can you think of any others?
12 Find out all you can about the disappearance of Richard III's nephews. What do you think happened to them? What evidence can you present to support your views? What is your own opinion of the character of Richard III?

The Publisher would like to thank the following for permission to reproduce photographs:

Malcolm Aird Associates Ltd (photo: Robert Estall), p.5(left); Bibliothèque Nationale, p.74; Bodleian Library, p.13, p.17, p.30(bottom) and p.31(right); British Library, p.14, p.24, p.75 and p.87; British Museum, p.51 and p.61; Vernon Brooke, p.35; Cambridge University Collection: copyright reserved, p.71; Charter Trustees of the town of King's Lynn (photo: Colin Shewring), p.39; Bruce Coleman Ltd, p.70(left) (photo: Jane Burton) and p.70(right) (photo: C James Webb); Master and Fellows of Corpus Christi College, Cambridge, p.33; Daily Telegraph Colour Library, p.12(middle left) (photo: John Marmaras) and p.12(middle right) (photo: Patrick Thurston); Guildhall Library, City of London, p.113(top); Holy Trinity Church, Stratford on Avon, pp.122−123(bottom) (photo: Holte); Kobal Collection, p.124(centre); Leeds United AFC, p.86; Manchester United FC, p.86; National Portrait Gallery, p.100 and p.124(left); National Trust, p.58; Oxford Mail and Times, p.12(top); Robert Pendreigh, p.81(top); Michael Poulton, pp.104−105, p.119, p.123(top) and p.124(top); Public Record Office (Crown copyright reserved), p.93; Ronald Sheridan, p.52; Society of Antiquaries, p.125(right); Alison Souster, pp.10−11, p.18 and p.81(bottom); Alan Spain, p.34(top); Syndication International, p.86(top); Jeffrey Tabberner, p.30(top); Dean and Chapter of Westminster Abbey, p.90(right) and p.125(left); Woodmansterne Ltd, p.5(right), p.31, p.90(left) and p.113(bottom); Geoffrey Wright, p.8.

Illustrations by Dick Barnard, Rudolph Britto, Norma Burgin, Michael Cole, Peter Dennis, Dan Escott, Oliver Frey, Richard Hook, John Hunt, Peter Kesteven, Gordon King, Christine Molan, Tony Morris, Michael Oakenfull, Ian Robertson and Colin Shearing.

The cover illustration, by Christine Molan, shows a Norman boy hunting with falcons.